M000196391

There are some pe[...]
so rare it is clearly [...]
hitting a golf ball or LeBron James playing bas-
ketball. Mike is one of those people. His ability
to bring words to life can only be explained as a
God-given talent and I've been honored to watch
him use his gifts for the glory of God. I have no
doubt you, too, will be blessed by his gift with
words as you read this book!

Joshua Gagnon, Lead Pastor of Next Level
Church and author of *It's Not Over*

Mike's humor shines through his telling of stories
from the Bible and his own life, making this an
enjoyable, refreshing book.

Tom Richter, Christian Speaker and Pastor
of Cullman First Baptist Church, Cullman, AL

Thrown Off Script offers a life-changing perspective shift. Stop feeling interrupted, and start seeing
opportunities!

Harris III, Storyteller, Master Illusionist

It's been an honor to know Mike for *many* years in
the local church context as well as at the national
level. Mike brings the same energy, humor, and
sincerity he radiates from stage, and crams it into
this book. Read it, and then read it again!

Wes Willis, lead singer, Rush Of Fools

THROWN OFF SCRIPT

Turn Interruptions Into Opportunities and Thrive in the Unexpected

MIKE DOMENY

AUTHOR
ACADEMY elite

Printed in the United States of America

Published by Author Academy Elite
PO Box 43, Powell, OH 43035 www.AuthorAcademyElite.com

ISBN: 978-1-64746-153-9 (paperback)
ISBN: 978-1-64746-154-6 (hardback)
ISBN: 978-1-64746-155-3 (e-book)

Library of Congress Control Number: 2020902958

Kelsey,
Your creativity and support have shaped not only this book, but me as a person. There is no one on earth with whom I'd rather walk this unscripted life. You are my teammate and best friend, and I'm so thankful for you.

Adalynne,
I am constantly amazed by your heart. I pray you will continue to give it to Jesus every day, and that you will find more and more opportunities to shine His light.

The author of my story, Jesus Christ,
If there's anything wise or clever or memorable in this book, or if there's anything that speaks to anyone's heart, it's because of You. I merely added some jokes.

CONTENTS

PART ONE
REDEFINING REAL LIFE

CHAPTER 1
THE ACTOR'S NIGHTMARE
The Pursuit of Predictability

I never intended to be an improv comedian. Not a bit. I enjoyed performing scripted theatre in high school and college, and I competed on my collegiate speech team, where I actively avoided the impromptu category. I graduated with a degree in Organizational Communication, which, though I'm still not sure what it means, promised to be more marketable than my minors in theatre, Bible, and psychology.

I had always been a type-A, predictability-seeking, five-minutes-early-is-five-minutes-late *non*-improviser. So, when my fiancée[*] and I still didn't have a job *three days before our wedding* (insert the anxious whimpers of two sets of parents understandably hesitant to give their blessing to this union) . . . needless to say, I felt stuck.

By God's grace (and undoubtedly countless late nights of internet-scouring on our behalf), my soon-to-be mother-in-law found a company hiring couples to travel the country and host school assemblies. It sounded like a scam, but hey, we were desperate. Literally one phone call with the hiring manager later, we were offered the job. Even though we didn't start for another month and weren't exactly sure what we'd be doing, the wedding went on with substantially more merriment.

A year went by, proving the job was indeed legitimate—we got paychecks and everything! My new wife and I genuinely cherished our first year as traveling assembly hosts, but the lifestyle of living out of a cargo van and loading and unloading equipment in and out of middle schools could only last so long.

As the year came to a close, I received an email out-of-the-blue, forwarded by a former professor. Another scam? It was from a Carl Crispin (sounded made-up), of 321 Improv (fake, probably), a national Christian improv comedy team (is that even a thing?). Two of the three guys were looking to retire from the team, and Carl

---

[*] She is now my wife. When she read this, she insisted I explain this refers to her and not some other woman. So here you go, honey.

(if that was indeed his real name) was reaching out through various channels to find replacements.

Improv? No thanks. The email sat in the inbox for a while. I could get a "real" job.

False. I could not. Faced with the decision either to commit to another year in the cargo van or try improv, I reached out to Carl. We had some good conversations, and I shared with him what little video footage I had of me on stage—a grainy clip of me with a sheet over my head as I shouted, "Oob!"—playing a ghost in a backward scene of Shakespeare's Hamlet, which should not have gotten me *any* job. But lo and behold, I was offered a role with 321 Improv.

That is . . . until Carl called a few weeks later, while my wife and I were literally driving our cargo van back to company headquarters to wrap up our tour.

"Hey, Mike, this is completely embarrassing, and I feel awful for having to even make this call . . . but the two guys decided they want to stay with 321. So, I regret that I have to take back the offer."

I was stunned. Was this some sort of improv test? To see how flexible I could be when plans changed? Maybe if I went along with it, he would say, "Whew! Nice job. I was only kidding. Life is improv, am I right? Have a good week—see you in Boca!"

But nope. It was for real. No job. No improv. And no time to find anything else. So, we called our company and asked for another year.

Over the course of the second year, God helped us realize a set-back can be a set-up. Our second year of travel was an even greater blessing than the first. We made friends with people across the country we cherish to this day, and we laid a foundation for our marriage which continues to be rewarding. We can settle an argument in ten minutes flat! When you spend two years in a van, there's nowhere to retreat when you're upset.

Fortunately, the start of my improv career was not completely lost. It was simply on hold. Carl's two team members finally decided one extra year was enough, and a spot became officially, irrevocably, mine.

In the weeks leading up to my first show with the team, I was a nervous wreck. Like I said, I had never really done improv. It was like being hired as a plumber without even knowing "righty-tighty, lefty-loosey."

I studied every 321 Improv video I could find—every game, every role, every interaction. I was determined to be the most prepared improviser in the history of improv!

But even after growing more comfortable with my role, I still couldn't escape the sense of inadequacy in my dreams. There's a phenomenon among performers called The Actor's Nightmare. Maybe you're familiar with it. It's a literal nightmare where the sleeping actor finds himself moments before going onstage without a clue about what to say, what to do, or who to be. Pants may or may not be present, but that's beside the point. The details of the dreams vary, of course, but all involve a sense of disorientation and having to grasp for sensible responses to everybody and everything. It can feel paralyzing.

I wish I could say, even today, such disorientation and panic has been confined to my dreams from which I can awaken, put on pants, and eat my yogurt and granola in peaceful predictability, but that's not the case.

Isn't real life a bit of an actor's nightmare? We must live with the reality that:

- **Life is unscripted.** There is no script to tell us the ideal things to do or say.
- **Consequences are unknown.** We cannot always anticipate the consequences of our words and actions.
- **The future is uncertain.** We cannot look pages ahead and know what will happen.
- **People are unpredictable.** They do not always act rationally and in a way convenient for us.
- **Impacts are unseen.** We may never become aware of the role we play in others' lives.

Living with the reality of those truths is easier said than done. When something unexpected occurs, we typically feel "thrown off" and react in one of four ways. Depending on when you react (*impulsive* or *delayed*), and where your focus is (*inward* or *outward*), you will probably relate strongly to one of these roles: The Analyzer, The Agonizer, The Arguer, and The Avoider.

The Analyzer (delayed and inward)

Have you heard the term "analysis paralysis"? The Analyzer has heard of it . . . and lives it. When faced with the unexpected, the Analyzer isn't comfortable moving forward until many possible actions have been explored. I have to raise my hand here and say this is me—if I'm not careful. To the Analyzer, thinking through options is considered wise. In making big life decisions, I would agree. But in reacting to the unexpected, the danger is the Analyzer spends so much time, well, *analyzing*, the moment passes, and opportunities are lost.

As an Analyzer . . .

- You believe there is a "best" choice to make, and you can figure it out if you have enough time.
- You try to predict the possible outcomes of several choices.
- You feel paralyzed because you "don't know what to do!"

The Agonizer (impulsive and inward)

Unlike the Analyzer, the Agonizer is often quick to react to a change of plans. Because of the nature of the job, or the Agonizer's personality, saying or doing something on the spot isn't the hard part. The real battle is fought afterward, inside the Agonizer's head.

As an Agonizer . . .

- You anguish over wondering if you did the right thing.
- You think negatively about yourself and how you wish you were better on your feet.
- You replay the situation many times over and come up with things you could have or should have said or done.

The Arguer (impulsive and outward)

The Arguer is the one heatedly interacting with the gate agent at the airport because of a canceled flight. The one holding up the line at the customer service desk. The verbally frustrated driver behind the car going five under the speed limit. The Arguer isn't always loud, and isn't even necessarily rude, but does expect someone else to change to get back to the way the Arguer believes things were or should be.

As an Arguer . . .

- You get frustrated when people don't act rationally.
- You blame others, or even God, for interrupting your plan.
- You prioritize getting back on track, even if it means stepping on other people's ideas and concerns.

The Avoider (delayed and outward)

The Avoider thinks the best way to deal with change is to ignore it. The Avoider may call this going with the flow, and there can be merit to that, but this very passive approach rarely experiences positive growth.

As an Avoider . . .

- You adopt an attitude of "whatever" to avoid having to deal with the issue.
- You doubt what you do and say even makes a difference.
- Ultimately, if a decision must be made, you let someone else make it.

If the description of any of these roles rings a bell, welcome to The Actor's Nightmare, my friend. The *bad* news is there's no waking up and no curtain falling to get you out of this nightmare. The *good* news is with a little reframing and retraining of your mind, you can not only survive these kinds of situations, you can thrive in them.

That's what improvisation is, at its heart. Take away the structure and predictability of a script and prepare yourself to respond in the moment to whatever comes your way.

And so, there is a *fifth* role you can learn to play in these situations. Ladies and gentlemen, I present to you . . .

The Improviser.

"Wait! That can't be right! It doesn't start with the letter *A*!" Unexpected, isn't it? Just testing you!

An Improviser understands it's not a question of *if* something unexpected will happen, but *when*. And when that time comes, the Improviser accepts the new reality and responds with what he or she trusts to be the next best step in the moment. This process continues until life's next curveball, and repeats.

As an Improviser . . .

- You have a "loose grip" on your plans and expectations.
- You view others as teammates whom you can support, and who can support you.
- You can respond effectively and move on.

Can you imagine having such an approach to life? Hopefully, you can, and that's why you're reading this book. By the end of our time together, you will have what you need to be an Improviser.

People will sometimes come up to me after an improv show and say, "Oh boy, I could never do what you do!" If they are referring to the fact that twenty minutes prior, I was acting like a mythological cross between a sloth and a llama (yes, you are correct: a sllama), I'd prescribe watching Animal Planet and spending some quality time in front of a mirror. But if they are referring to the whole making stuff up as you go thing, then I have to ask, "In a way, aren't we all improvising?"

The truth is, we are all thrust out on this stage called life and given a general expectation of what we're supposed to accomplish. When you think you have an idea of where you're headed—surprise! As in an improv scene, a 1973 Buick LeSabre drives through your kitchen window (okay, I hope that *only* happens in an improv scene).

Your scene may be your ministry, your workplace, your family, or your relationships. Interruptions pop up daily as reminders you can't be ready for everything. A flat tire on the way to work. A new project with an unreasonably short deadline. A phone call from someone who needs your help— now! And sometimes, something unexpected happens to turn the scene into a nightmare. An unfortunate change in employment or relation- ship status. A sickness. Surprise bills. We cannot, of course, change these circumstances. We can, however, change our reaction to them.

Just like improvising musicians can't play what- ever random notes they want and call it jazz, we can't say or do whatever we want and call it improv. As off-the-cuff as improv appears, there are actu- ally quite a few principles and rules the actors follow to keep things moving forward and avoid getting stuck. These principles, when applied to your real, unscripted life, help you do the same.

To start, let's look at the life of a man whose responses to interruptions didn't merely keep things moving forward but had an impact on hun- dreds and thousands of people and generations to come—the Master Improviser, Jesus.

CHAPTER 2
A MINISTRY OF INTERRUPTIONS

Jesus, Master Improviser

Imagine you're in a conference room, and you're giving an important presentation on, say, the avocado industry. The place is packed. Not only are the twelve leather seats around the table occupied, but people are standing around the perimeter of the room, at times two or three bodies deep. It's mid-summer and the air conditioning has been fluky lately, so people are tugging at their ties, fanning their faces with their papers, and shifting their weight uncomfortably.

Despite this, you remain focused. You are casting vision, your charts and graphs show growth, your list of avaca*dos* and avaca*don'ts* is received with genuine chuckles, until—what's that?—you hear some unusual clanging sounds coming from the ceiling. Somebody needs to call the air conditioning guy—again. You continue speaking. Bits of foam and insulation fall like snow onto your nose. The drop-down ceiling tiles begin to sway until the one above your head cracks in two and a lunchbox full of—are those avocados?—is lowered into the room, right in front of you!

Everyone in the room gasps. Is this part of the presentation? What's more, two colleagues poke their heads through the hole in the ceiling, shouting,

"Hey, it's Rod and Terry from accounting! We tried calling, but the receptionist said you were busy. We packed these avocados as snacks, but we think they're diseased. Can you check on them for us?

Crazy, right? Talk about an unexpected interruption! Believe it or not, Jesus found himself in this exact situation!* And when you look at the accounts of Jesus' life on earth, it seems like interruptions

---

* Except, it was nearly two thousand years ago, and instead of a presentation, Jesus was teaching about God's kingdom; instead of a conference room with a drop-down ceiling, it was a single-story abode with a flat, plaster roof; and instead of a lunchbox full of avocados, it was a paralyzed man. Rod and Terry were this man's friends and not from accounting, but they could have been named Rod and Terry—we can't prove they weren't. Otherwise, yeah, it was the same thing. Check out Luke 5:17-19.

happened more often than not. In fact, His ministry is practically made of one disruption after the next. Walk with me through a couple chapters of the book of Luke, and I'll show you what I mean.

Jesus, the Relationship-Builder

(Luke 8:22-25)

After a long day of teaching, Jesus gathered His closest friends and said, "Let's cross to the other side of the lake."

Now, this alone may have put His disciples a bit on edge. On the "other side" of the lake was the Gerasene region. It was home to non-Jews, and a devout Jew would not risk associating with the "other side" for fear of being unclean, but Jesus was tired, and that's what He wanted to do, so His friends obliged.

Regardless of what awaited them on the other side, the trip itself offered something Jesus desired: sleep.

He had celebrity status at this point. Crowds followed Him wherever He went. When He tried to find an isolated place to rest, hordes of people went searching for Him until they found Him. So, for Jesus, what was the best way to avoid the first century paparazzi? Hop in a boat with some friends and retreat to the middle of the lake.

His friends handled the sails, but as Jesus settled in for a nap, a storm settled right on top of them—a bad one, even for experienced fishermen who grew up on the lake. The storm was a major, life-threatening interruption for the disciples. Assuming the mission to "the other side" was already questionable in their minds, the storm must have felt like confirmation they made the wrong decision.

Agonizer disciples wished they had never left the shore or had spoken up sooner. "I knew this was a bad idea."

Arguer disciples looked around for Jesus. "Where is He? Why isn't He helping us get out of this?" They looked over and found Him asleep on a cushion. I can picture them shaking Him out of His sleep.* "Don't you care that we're going to drown?" (Mark 4:38).

Jesus did, in fact, care. But they weren't going to drown. Even though the storm instigated this whole turn of events, it was not the core issue. What was the core issue? The disciples' lack of faith. They were scared and struggling. Jesus saw through the circumstances and focused on the people involved.

> **Jesus saw through the circumstances and focused on the people involved.**

The storm didn't interrupt Jesus. His disciples did. Jesus took a moment to calm the storm not for His sake, but for His disciples. With the storm out of the way, Jesus' friends were in a position to listen. Jesus asked poignantly, "Where is your faith?" Understand, the strength of the disciples'

---

* I've been married for several years now, and one thing I've learned is if I wake up my wife, the storm is just about to begin. Just saying.

faith depended on how much they trusted Jesus was who He said He was. They couldn't control the storm, but they could control their belief. Jesus was more concerned with their relationship than the circumstances, so that became the focus when interruptions arose. *Jesus was a relationship-builder.*

Jesus, the Problem-Solver

(Luke 8:26-39)

The journey was completed on calm seas, and the men arrived in the Gerasene region. Remember, the disciples were already nervous about "the other side" of the lake. The Jews believed those residents were unholy, unsociable, unclean weirdos.

Literally, "as Jesus was climbing out of the boat," who should interrupt their arrival other than a demon-possessed (unholy), homeless and naked (unsociable) man who lived in the graveyard (unclean), howled, and cut himself with stones (weirdo).

Have you ever arrived at work, a party, church, a reunion—wherever—and no sooner do you finish thinking, "Please don't let him be here . . . please don't let him see me," than you are greeted by "that guy" at the dad-gum door?

You can almost feel the Avoider disciples rolling their eyes and scurrying to get back in the boat as this abomination of a man approached them. "Uh . . . let Jesus handle this one." Well, that's exactly what He did.

I don't need to go into all the details here. You can read the account for yourself. Jesus cast out the demon, which turned out to be thousands of demons. Pigs were involved; they ran off a cliff. It was a whole big thing. Here's the point:

The man had a big problem, and it was not that he was homeless, naked, lived in a graveyard, howled, and cut himself. It was that demons tormented him. The other things were simply the obvious, visual symptoms. Locals tried to restrain this guy with chains and shackles, but every time, the demonic man overpowered them, broke the bonds holding him, and ran off into the wilderness.

Jesus cut right to the cause and addressed the man's real problem. With a word, the demons fled. Then, Jesus could properly tend to the remaining symptoms.

When the people from the town came over to check out what all the commotion was about, Luke says they found the man "sitting at Jesus' feet, fully clothed and perfectly sane." Apparently, Jesus and His friends shared their clothing with him. Jesus then instructed him, "Go back to your family and tell them everything God has done for you."

Jesus exorcised the man's demons (no longer unholy). He clothed the man and reconciled his relationship with his family (no longer unsociable). He reinstated him into society (no longer unclean) and restored the man's sanity (no longer a weirdo).

Handymen know if a leak is causing water damage to the drywall, the first step is not to replace the drywall. Mechanics know filling a punctured tire with air won't ultimately do any good until the hole is patched. Jesus recognized repairing symptoms would not do any lasting good until He fixed the cause. *Jesus was a problem-solver.*

Jesus, the Pace-Setter

(Luke 8:40-48)

Apparently, the residents of the Gerasene region were a bit freaked out by the cliff-diving demon-pig episode, so they begged Jesus to leave. He and the disciples sailed *back* across the lake (much to the relief of the disciples, I'm sure), where they found a huge crowd waiting for them on the shore (much to their dismay).

Have you ever returned home after a long day of work to find your household in need of . . . well . . . you? The toilet is clogged, a lasagna is burning in the oven, someone is crying (spouse or child, or both), and it is clear this is not going to be the haven you hoped it would be. Your day is not yet done.

Neither was Jesus'. His feet barely touched land before a man named Jairus fell at them. Jairus' only daughter was on her deathbed, and Jairus begged Jesus to come to his house to heal her.

In the disciples' minds, this was an emergency. Time was running out. They took on Jairus' panic as their own. I picture Peter as a big, physical guy, leading the pack, and elbowing his way through the crowd. Brothers James and John, living up to their nickname, "Sons of Thunder," were probably playing the first-century equivalent of an ambulance and shouting, "Make way!" "Healer coming through!" and "WEE-OOO, WEE-OOO!"

But Jesus did not let Himself get caught up in the rush of the moment. Simply because someone approached Him with their emergency did not make it His emergency. As Jesus' disciples pressed through the crowd, the crowd continued to press against Jesus. People surrounded him. But Jesus stopped and focused on only one.

"Who touched me?" He asked.

> **Simply because someone approached Him with their emergency did not make it His emergency.**

Imagine the baffled look on the faces of the disciples. Jesus was being touched by practically everybody around Him.

Peter even said, "Master, this whole crowd is pressing up against you!"

Jairus, I'm sure, was panicking, "What's the hold up? My daughter's dying!"

But because Jesus was controlling His own pace, it allowed Him to be able to pause and address *another* interruption. That's right, even Jesus' interruptions were interrupted! This time, it was by a woman who had been bleeding for twelve years. This meant she was considered to be unclean by Jewish law. She believed if she could at least touch Jesus' robe as He walked by, it would be enough to heal her, and she could slip away again unnoticed.

Well, she was right about one thing. A simple touch was enough. She was healed instantly. But slip away unnoticed? Not so much. When Jesus stopped and brought attention to the fact He was touched, she realized she couldn't remain anonymous, so she spoke up.

Luke wrote, "The whole crowd heard her explain why she had touched him and that she had been immediately healed."

Did you catch that? The *whole crowd* heard her—the same crowd that only minutes earlier was jostling and pressing up against Jesus trying to get His attention. The pace of the disciples and the crowd slowed to match Jesus. He helped them arrive at a position where they could begin to listen. *Jesus was a pace-setter.*

Jesus, the Truth-Teller

(Luke 8:49-56)

Check out the transition here in verse 49: "While he was still speaking to her . . ."

So, for those of you keeping score at home, this is an interruption of an interruption of an interruption! What happened? It didn't look good.

Someone from Jairus' house came and found him and reported, sadly, Jairus' daughter died, and he shouldn't trouble Jesus anymore. But Jesus wasn't troubled, and He encouraged Jairus not to worry, either. "Don't be afraid. Just have faith, and she will be healed."

Healed? You heard the messenger, right? She died. She's literally dead. Jesus arrived at the house to find it filled with family and friends, all weeping.

Agonizer disciples were probably thinking "Guh! If we hadn't stopped to deal with that bleeding lady, we would have made it!" "If we had just run a little faster, Jesus would have been here in time!"

But Jesus didn't acknowledge any of it. Instead, He focused on what was true. He said, "Stop the weeping! She isn't dead; she's only asleep."

Okay, it was true she died. Everyone there could confirm that. But they didn't have the complete picture. What was *really* true was her death was not final, and Jesus could bring her back from the dead. He could, and He would. Jesus told the girl to get up, and, to everyone's amazement, she did.

Jesus' response was based on what He knew to be true. Not what *could* be true, not what He *wished* was true, not what *appeared* to be true. What He *knew* to be true. *Jesus was a truth-teller.*

What a day, huh? Of course, Jesus was interrupted countless other times—for example, while He was . . .

- at dinner (Luke 7:36)
- having a conversation (Luke 12:11-21)
- praying (Mark 1:35-37)
- teaching (Luke 4:33-35)
- visiting a friend (Luke 4:38)
- resting (Luke 4:42)
- sleep-deprived (Luke 6:12-19)
- at a wedding (John 2:1-12)
- and grieving (Matthew 14:13-21)

... to name a few. In fact, I'd like to zoom in on the last one in Matthew to make some final points and lay the foundation for the rest of our conversation.

Jesus, the Action-Taker

(Matthew 14:15-19)

Jesus had heard some devastating news. His cousin, John the Baptist, was murdered by the region's ruler. In an attempt to grieve in peace, Jesus withdrew by boat to the middle of the lake. Remember, this seemed to be the most effective way to escape the large crowds. Well, these crowds heard about His retreat, so they gathered on the shore and waited for Him to return.

When He did, they wasted no time in asking for His services, and He wasted no time in offering them. As evening set in, Jesus was still healing and teaching. His disciples gauged the atmosphere of the crowd and saw the people were hungry and restless. They suggested Jesus call it a day and send them back to the village, but He had a better idea.

"They do not need to go away. You give them something to eat."

Blank stares. A look over at the crowd of nearly five thousand families. Blank stares back at Jesus. Jesus sent His skeptical disciples to take inventory of how many loaves of bread were nearby. Their report was laughable. "Five."

Five loaves of bread. I don't know, then, if they were genuinely trying to be helpful, or if it was a bit sarcastic, but they added, ". . . and two fish."

Here's where many of us would get stuck in this situation. *Analyzers* would mentally race through options. "Do we send them home? Do we buy food?" etc. *Arguers*, no doubt fueled a bit by their own hunger, would direct their complaints toward those who got them in this position—the crowd, for staying too late; the other disciples, for not seeing the problem sooner; even Jesus, for not sending the crowd away.

Agonizers, on the other hand, would feel personally responsible for the lack of dinner, and *Avoiders* would throw their hands up in surrender and let the others figure it out for themselves.

Honestly, Jesus could have fed the crowd any number of ways. He had the power, but He chose to use what was already available and make the best of it. "Bring them here to me," Jesus said, and thus began one of the most famous miracles in Jesus' ministry.

Jesus was an action-taker. He took the food He had, broke off bits of bread and fish and . . . kept breaking off more! He handed the pieces off to the disciples, who served the crowd until all five thousand families had their fill. But wait! There's more. . .

Jesus, the All-Giver

(Matthew 14:20-21)

Twelve basketfuls more, to be exact. Not only did every family receive *something* to eat, they ate and were satisfied, Matthew said. And not only was everyone satisfied, there were *left-overs*! Do you realize how all-in Jesus went on this miracle? It would have been a miracle to satisfy *fifty* people with the food Jesus started with. But to go beyond and have something for everyone, and then to go beyond even that and give them *more* than they could eat? That's some high-level commitment to the task! *Jesus was an all-giver.*

It shouldn't be surprising, really. Jesus forecasted this total commitment to His mission early on in His ministry:

> For I have come down from heaven to do the will of God who sent me, not to do my own will. And this is the will of God, that *I should not lose even one of all those he has given me*, but that I should raise them up at the last day. For it is my Father's will that *all* who see his Son and believe in him should have eternal life." (John 3:38-40, emphasis mine)

It's what healed entire crowds. It's what fed the five thousand. It's what held Him to the cross.

We've seen Jesus, the Master Improviser, respond to numerous interruptions by taking on the roles of

- *Relationship-Builder*
- *Problem-Solver*
- *Pace-Setter*
- *Truth-Teller*
- *Action-Taker*
- *All-Giver*

If we are to be skilled improvisers in this unscripted life, these traits must be true of us.

Okay, Mike. I get it. But how? I'm not Jesus.

Fair point. Let me answer by pulling out one key detail from the last story. Mark gives us an especially important insight into the mindset of Jesus—a mindset we must make our own if we want any success in navigating the unexpected in life.

Remember, before Jesus fed the crowd, He had recently come from solitary time on the lake grieving the death of His cousin. Put yourself in Jesus' shoes (well, sandals). How would you react to seeing a crowd of people wanting your attention? *Are you kidding me? Not them again. Don't they even care about how I feel? I'm so exhausted.* Nobody would blame you for thinking those things. But check this out.

"When Jesus landed and saw a large crowd, he had compassion on them, because they were like sheep without a shepherd" (Mark 6:34).

How did Jesus deal with interruptions? *He didn't view them as interruptions!* He considered each interruption *an opportunity* to show compassion, to love, to shepherd. These were not interruptions to His real life. They *were* His real life.

The same is true of you. It's time for a paradigm shift.

CHAPTER 3
A NEW REALITY

Turning Interruptions into Opportunities

In 2018, my wife Kelsey and I produced a comedy called *Fruitcake: A Deliciously Nutty Christmas Mash-Up.* The play highlighted three high-energy actors in their quest to portray every aspect of the Christmas season in one hilarious, sugar-rush of a show. They performed renditions of seasonal favorites such as *A Christmas Carol, The Nutcracker, Frosty the Snowman,* and more through sword-fighting, reggae, rap, ballet, improvisation, poetry, and over a hundred props and costumes. Kelsey and I wrote it; she directed it. It was the product of years of work, and the capstone project of our theatre experience.

Three days before opening night, we told our actors to break a leg. So, one did. Literally. She landed on her ankle wrong during a rehearsal of the sword fight scene in The Nutcracker, and everything came to a screeching halt.

We cancelled the rest of rehearsal, and Kelsey took the actor to urgent care to determine if she could get by with a walking cast, or if she needed crutches. We prayed hard for the boot. The show was extremely physical, so if the actor had two hands busy operating the crutches, and one bad foot, there didn't seem to be any way to proceed with the show without some major rehaul. A walking boot would at least free up the actor enough to do most of what she had practiced.

After a grueling hour waiting for the prognosis, we had our answer. The doctor didn't seem to care that "the show must go on." It would have to go on, apparently, on crutches.

The dismaying turn of events forced the next seventy-two-hours into an all-hands-on-deck brainstorming session. Before we got into the details of what would have to change, and especially before depression and regret sank into the cast and crew, I took a moment to cast some vision.

"This is the show now, and it's a great show."

Whether we said them aloud or not, we were all thinking similar (negative) thoughts:

The show was going to be so good!

The show won't be the same with someone on crutches!
People are going to worry about her.
I wish people could have seen what it was before this happened.

The interruption to our plans bumped us not-so-gently onto another road, to be sure. But our thoughts were born by looking over the median at where we used to be and where we could have been if we didn't get shoved off. If we kept our vision set on what used to be but isn't, and what could have been but can't be, we would be useless where we were.

So, I said to the group, "This is *Fruitcake* now. This is not worse than *Fruitcake*; we're not calling this *Plan B Fruitcake*; this isn't even a different *Fruitcake*. This *is Fruitcake*. And we're going forward as if this was the plan all along. This is the show now, and it's a great show."

With that perspective, we were free to brainstorm how to make the most of one of our actors being on crutches. We added some related jokes to her monologue at the top of the show to acknowledge the injury and put the audience at ease. We invented some funny business involving a rolling office chair as a means of getting around. And, to the audience's delight, we integrated a stunt double—a fourth actor introduced in the beginning and called in at various points to perform the most physical tasks.

The feedback we received was comments like, "I wasn't sure if the broken leg was real or not!"

"That stunt double seemed like it was written into the show all along!" "You should keep the stunt double in the script!"

People didn't feel like they were watching a salvaged show, or a good show given the circumstances. They were experiencing *the show*.

This is the show now became our mantra. It needed to be repeated in order to stick. It was an exciting opportunity, and not a melancholy reminder, so we always added, *and it's a great show!* And that's exactly what it became.

Is this real life?

Your show may be your plan, your project, or your routine. In a general sense, your life is your show. But as long as you consider your life as your *real* life, or even *your* life in the first place, interruptions and the unexpected will continue to be a source of frustration and anxiety. C.S. Lewis offers a re-definition of real life:

> The great thing, if one can, is to stop regarding all the unpleasant things as interruptions of one's 'own' or one's 'real' life. The truth is of course that what one calls interruptions are precisely one's real life—the life God is sending one day by day; what one calls one's real life is a phantom of one's imagination. [1]

Interruptions. Obstacles. The unexpected. These don't *derail* your life. Life doesn't wait to resume when they're over. They *are* your life. As such, *the way you treat your interruptions is how you treat your life*. You can live a life full of frustration and helplessness, or you can live a life full of *opportunities*. Interruptions are opportunities to grow, connect, and discover plans much more impactful than yours. The bigger the interruption, the bigger the opportunity. If an

> **The way you treat your interruptions is how you treat your life.**

interruption inconveniences only you, then it's an opportunity for you to grow a little closer to God. If the interruption affects more people, so can your response to it.

In 2018, the band Rush Of Fools was performing at a national youth ministry conference in Chattanooga, Tennessee. Their worship set was interrupted by the sound of the fire alarm ripping through the auditorium. A couple thousand youth ministers remembered their fire drill training from elementary school and filtered out to the opposite sidewalk.

Unfortunately, there was indeed a small fire that started in the kitchen, so the conference could not resume its regularly scheduled programming. Rush Of Fools recognized this interruption not as an obstacle, but as an opportunity. They strapped on their acoustic guitars and proceeded to lead all within earshot into an impromptu sidewalk worship experience.

Later, people in attendance said it was the most powerful worship experience they had ever witnessed. By embracing the opportunity, the band was able to realign their own hearts to God's plan. Furthermore, their leadership set an example for the crowd (many of whom were likely disoriented, frustrated, or impatient) to recognize God's invitation in the situation and align their hearts with His.

If *opportunities to embrace God's plan* is the what, then *to align our hearts and minds to God's* is the why. A closer relationship with God is why Jesus came in the first place, and why God continues to allow interruptions to come into our life. Dietrich Bonhoeffer wrote in *Life Together,*

> We must be ready to allow ourselves to be interrupted by God. God will be constantly crossing our paths and canceling our plans by sending us people with claims and petitions. We may pass them by, preoccupied with our more important tasks... It is a strange fact that Christians and even ministers frequently consider their work so important and urgent that they will allow nothing to disturb them. They think they are doing God a service in this, but actually they are disdaining God's "crooked yet straight path."[2]

The crooked yet straight path.

At first, this phrase looks like an oxymoron. How can something be crooked yet straight? But anybody who has been trail hiking knows how you can be on the path that ultimately leads to your destination but is certainly not easy or straightforward. I'll do you one better, though.

Starting on our honeymoon and extending into the second year of our marriage, my wife and I were particularly into spelunking (cave exploration, for the uninitiated). Okay, I'm making us sound way more off-the-grid than we really were. We overpaid a bunch of times for tours of a bunch of caves in Missouri and nearby states. The one time we did enter a cave not on a tour, we backed out after a few minutes because, you know, it got dark.

Anyway, adjacent to the parking lot at Talking Rocks Cavern in Branson, Missouri is a wooden structure that from the outside looks rather unassuming and even fun. It even has a fun name: The Speleobox. But don't let its pleasant, wood-slatted exterior fool you. Inside this shed-sized cave simulator is a 150-foot maze of torso-twisting, back-breaking, and shin-scraping passageways that make you feel like you are personally impacting the intestine of the Trojan Horse.

The sign at the entrance said the course is not for people over 6' 2" or 230 pounds. I'm 5' 10" and 140 pounds, and my wife, too, is well under the limit (see how I did that? Men, take note), so we dove in whole-heartedly.

After twenty-eight hours* of shimmying shoulders and channeling our inner (non-existent) contortionists, we emerged from the sole exit, which so happened to be three ironic feet from the hole where we entered.

Thanks to Speleobox, I have a vivid understanding of *crooked, yet straight*. With all the switch-backs and corkscrews and narrow, 90-degree turns, the path was extremely crooked. The only comfort (and I do mean *only* comfort) was knowing going forward was the right way to go (not that we had a choice).

When you imagine your life as an interruption-free ideal, it looks like a straight road. If something makes you turn right or left, you feel off-road, and you try desperately to get back on track. What God offers is the peace of mind to know that no matter how crooked it may feel, the path leads straight to Him.

A Loose Grip.

"So, Mike, where does making plans fit in all of this? Are you saying we shouldn't make any plans?"

I knew this question would come up! No, I'm not suggesting we don't make plans—in a life sense, or even in an improv sense. Believe it or not, improvisers have a plan. The scene only works, though, when the improvisers have a *loose grip*

---

* Could have been fifteen minutes. It likely was. Time has no meaning when you're fighting for survival.

on their plan. This is the middle ground between having no plan and having a *tight* grip on a plan.

Let me show you the difference in the context of improv and then what the Bible has to say about the issue.

If an improviser has no plan, the scene will start something like this:

"Hi."

Or for the more verbose actor, "Hey, whatcha doing?"

Starting a scene this way puts the pressure on the other actor to single-handedly create the essential elements of what makes a scene: character, context, relationship, etc. If the scene partner doesn't pick up all the pieces, the scene falls flat. Fast.

The other extreme is equally frustrating for the other actors:

"Mr. Musk, can I call you Elon? I never thought when I applied for this internship that I'd end up on the golf course with you! While you chip your ball out of the sand trap, could you elaborate further on your plans to open a coffee shop on Mars?"

If one actor has a grand elaborate plan for how the scene should go, the other actors are forced to fit into it and are robbed of creativity. There's an old improv adage that says, *Bring a brick, not a cathedral.* I'll elaborate more on this in Chapter 11, but it's too good to not share now. Bring a brick, not a cathedral. Don't come empty-handed into a scene on stage or a scene in life. But also, don't bring a fully-constructed cathedral with pews engraved with names of patrons, stained-glass windows depicting historical events, and every slate roof tile securely in place.

Bring a brick. Maybe yours will be the first brick, around which will be built a fire station, a school, or maybe even a cathedral that somewhat resembles the idea in your head. Maybe your brick helps someone else's idea become a reality.

Whatever the case, the result will be one for which you cannot take sole credit, and which represents the combined creativity and will of many others.

Bringing a brick, not a cathedral, means having a loose grip on your plans. It's a grip that is ready and willing to work and will contribute when it looks like progress is being made in another direction.

The Bible reminds us of the importance of keeping a loose grip on our plans in Proverbs 16:9. "We can make our plans, but the Lord determines our steps." We can make our plans (a grip), but the Lord determines our steps (a loose grip).

James offers some advice on how to keep the loose grip mentality:

"Now listen, you who say, 'Today or tomorrow we will go to this or that city, spend a year there, carry on business and make money.' Why, you do not even know what will happen tomorrow. What is your life? You are a mist that appears for a little while and then vanishes. Instead, you ought to say, 'If it is the Lord's will, we will live and do this or that'" (James 4:13-15 (NIV).

If we go about our lives disregarding the facts (1) we don't know our future, and (2) God's will may be different than ours, then we are setting ourselves up for disappointment and frustration when things don't go according to our plan. If it's the Lord's will, we will live and do this or that. A loose grip acknowledges God's sovereignty to interrupt our plans.

God *has* to interrupt us. If we were to sail through life according to our plan, then we could pat ourselves on the back for planning so well. We wouldn't have any need to interact with Him, and He wouldn't receive any glory for any good thing. Instead, He injects our path with unexpected people and events in the hope that in each of those instances, we turn to Him for wisdom, strength, and with the expectation that He will be glorified.

Take a look at Paul's resumé of interruptions, formed over years of grueling missionary work:

> Five times I received from the Jews the forty lashes minus one. Three times I was beaten with rods, once I was pelted with stones, three times I was shipwrecked, I spent a night and a day in the open sea, I have been constantly on the move. I have been in danger from rivers, in danger from bandits, in danger from my fellow Jews, in danger from Gentiles; in danger in the city, in danger in the country, in danger at sea; and in danger from false believers. I have labored and toiled and have often gone without sleep; I have known hunger and thirst and have often gone without food; I have been cold and naked. (2 Corinthians 11:24-27)

Talk about things not exactly going smoothly and according to plan! He goes on to describe a "thorn," some sort of constantly-aggravating disturbance he admits God allowed to bother him to keep him from being conceited. He begged God three separate times to take away this interruption.

> But He said to me, "My grace is sufficient for you, for my power is made perfect in weakness." Therefore, I will boast all the more gladly about my weaknesses, so that Christ's power may rest on me. That is why, for Christ's sake, I delight in weaknesses, in insults, in hardships, in persecutions, in difficulties. For when I am weak, then I am strong. (2 Corinthians 12:9-10)

When our plans get interrupted and when life takes an unexpected turn, we feel out of control. We feel weak. The reality is we were never in control, and we *are*, in fact, weak. But the good news is we have the opportunity to be made stronger in our weakness.

This process of being made stronger can only be initiated and completed by God. It requires us to recognize "real life" is the one God gives us day by day, crooked path and all. It requires us to keep a "loose grip" on our plans, and to recognize interruptions as opportunities to draw closer to Him and help others do the same.

This book is not here to help you deal with interruptions so you can get back to the way you want things to be. If that's still what you're hoping to get out of it, then thank you for reading up to this point and you're welcome to continue, but you won't find those answers here (or, dare I say, anywhere).

Rather, I believe a truly fulfilling life—one defined by joy and peace instead of frustration and anxiety—can be found by recognizing interruptions as Jesus' call to a closer relationship with Him. That's the foundation of this book, which we have now established in Section 1. The rest of the book will provide tips and tricks from improv about *how* to do that.

Ahead, each chapter will focus on one key element of improv. Section 2 contains the fundamental ideas you would be taught in any Improv 101 class across the country. Section 3 contains several hand-picked principles of improv about how to make a scene, and by extension your life, particularly vibrant. Ready? Let's do it.

PART TWO

AN IMPROV-ED APPROACH TO LIFE

CHAPTER 4

LISTEN UP!

The Art of Listening and Responding

The single most common fear I hear from people who are hesitant to try improv is, "I wouldn't know what to say!" It comes as a surprise to them the first lesson in improv actually has nothing to do with saying anything.

The hardest improv game for me is what I call Mr. Know-it-All. When 321 Improv plays this game, we take a question from an audience member looking for advice of some kind. Then we answer the question, taking turns as we respond one word at a time. As you can imagine, we are each subject to the whims of the other two, as one word can derail the direction of the sentence drastically. I usually have an idea of where I'd like to take the sentence if I have the chance, but I can't respond with "Chocolate!" simply because it's my turn to speak.

Success in this game—in improv in general and in life even more generally—hinges not on the response, but on listening to what is given.

Improv has been dubbed the art of listening and responding. The same can be said of an improv-ed life. But without listening, you are merely responding *with*. You respond *with* the reason the other person is mistaken. You respond *with* the sarcastic comeback you thought of, or *with* a joke when the mood isn't right. You respond *with* an eye roll and leave the room.

But when you listen before responding, you know what you are responding *to*. You can respond *to* a concern that's been raised. You can respond *to* a misunderstanding. You can respond *to* the pain someone is feeling.

Are you responding *with* or responding *to*?

Responding *with* requires thinking while the other person is talking
Responding *to* requires listening while the other person is talking.

Responding *with* means having an answer ready.
Responding *to* means understanding the question.

Responding *with* means having a tight grip on where the conversation will go.
Responding *to* means having a loose grip on where the conversation *could* go.

Responding *with* can interrupt.
Responding *to* cannot interrupt.

Responding *with* is quick to speak.
Responding *to* is quick to listen.

Quick to listen.

"Understand this," says James, the brother of Jesus. "You must all be quick to listen, slow to speak and slow to become angry" (James 1:19).

How can you be quick to listen? Doesn't it . . . I don't know . . . simply *happen*? You're probably thinking of hearing. Hearing does happen for those who are able. Listening is a skill and a discipline that, like any other, can be developed and improved.

Listening is so important to relationships and communication that there is an actual International Listening Association. The ILA shared an interview with Dr. Ralph Nichols, The Father of the Field of Listening. He was asked, "What do you consider your most significant accomplishment in the field of listening?"

He replied, "I'm sorry . . . what was the question again?"

I'm kidding. That would have been awesome. Actually, he answered with the fundamental discovery that listening can be taught.

If listening can be taught, then we must learn it. According to Dr. Nichols, listening addresses people's most basic need. "The most basic of human needs is the need to understand and be understood. The best way to understand people is to listen to them."[1]

Understand and be understood. Stephen Covey, author of *7 Habits of Highly Effective People*, prescribes them in this order. "Seek first to understand, and then to be understood."[2]

This lesson is such a fundamental one to master. It doesn't matter who you are; being a better listener makes you a more effective friend, spouse, parent, employee, manager—whatever role you play, listening will make you better at it. But since I believe the benefits of becoming a better follower of Jesus will trickle down to all those other areas, let's talk about improving listening in a relationship with Christ. Of course, feel free to apply these principles to other relationships, as well.

Tune In.

Through traveling with 321 Improv, I've gotten to witness many bands' soundchecks before the event. Some go on for well over an hour. The output for each instrument, each drum and cymbal, and each voice is adjusted for the optimal mix of sound. The painstaking process is laughable when juxtaposed with our sound check. Three guys. Three headset microphones.

"Carl?"

"Check, check. A, B, C, D."

"Good. Mike?"

"Microphone check. This is Mike's mic."

"Good. Jeremy?"

"Hello, all you beautiful empty chairs out there."

"Good. All set."

And then we head back to the green room for pita chips and hummus, but not before giving a wink and a thumbs up to the band, who will continue to make adjustments right until the event doors open.

For the bands, though, the sound check is not primarily for the benefit of the audience. It's for themselves. Each band member wears an in-ear monitor. Each musician's sound is transmitted to the audio engineer, who controls a mixer to adjust the volume of each instrument and voice as it's played into each in-ear monitor.

It's an interesting process to watch. The electric guitarist will play solo, and the other band members will point up if they want more guitar volume in their ears or point down if they want less. The audio engineer adjusts the levels of the track for each musician. When everyone is happy with the level of the electric guitar, they repeat the process with the next instrument, and so on. In the end, each musician will have a mix in their ear according to what they want to hear. A vocalist may want louder keyboard and backup vocals, but quieter bass guitar. The electric guitarist may want louder drums and hardly any vocals at all.

When the mix is right for the band, they can play in harmony and the audience can enjoy the sound. When the mix is off, it creates confusion.

And here's the key to active listening: You control the mix. You control the volume of the input.

Try this. For the next minute, listen to what is going on around you. Try to separate each source of noise in your mind. I'll play along, too. As I write this, I'm in a hotel room. The air conditioner fan is whirring. It's gusty outside, so I hear the effects of the wind. There's a busy road outside my window, so I hear the cars pass. And finally, I have smooth jazz playing from my phone (it's my go-to writing music).

What about you? What sounds are going on around you? Once you've identified some, play with the mixer in your mind to amplify one of the "tracks." The louder sounds are easy. Try to hone in on a quieter one.

You control the mix. You control the volume of the input.

A bit trickier, isn't it? But the more you focus on the quiet sound, doesn't it seem to get louder? You become much more aware of its existence.

You control the mix. This is the difference between hearing and listening. You *hear* everything that enters your ear canal (or crosses your mind). You *listen* to what you choose to amplify. Choose wisely.

Clear the Mechanism.

In the movie *For Love of the Game*, Kevin Costner played Billy Chapel, a once-great baseball pitcher at the end of his career. Billy struggled in his final season amidst a losing record, a nagging injury, and a distressed personal life. Even in the middle of a game, these self-defeating thoughts and regrets consumed his mind to the point he was unaware he was pitching a perfect game. When he realized the situation, the external voices became louder.

The closer he got to victory, the more the hecklers bore down on him.

"You're done! You're finished! Get out of town! You couldn't pitch a tent!"

The deafening voices, both internal and external, were jeopardizing Billy's ability to get the job done until he reminded himself of his mantra, *Clear the mechanism*. With those three words, the roar of the crowd became a whisper. His vision focused. He could give his full attention to his catcher. The last batter struck out, and the perfect game was complete.

Clear the mechanism. Negative voices will *litter* (because they are put there) and *clutter* (because you leave them there) your mechanism, your mind, as each competes to be the loudest voice in your head.

Deceit, discouragement, distractions, and doubts bombard you daily. The more you dwell on them, the louder they get. The louder they get, the less you can hear anything else. And then, my friend, you'll find yourself caught in a private conversation that will render you ineffective.

Deceit.

You have a very real enemy who wants to cripple your ability to be close to God, and physically kill you to remove you from this earth. That's not fun to say in a book based on improv comedy, but it needs to be acknowledged. When life presses down hard, Satan is quick to swoop in to try to convince you that you are alone. If you have thoughts like, *I can do this without God* or *God must not care what's happening*, those are lies straight from Satan, and they are the oldest trick in the book (literally).

Discouragement.

There's something about discouragement that seems to stick around. Something somebody said to you years ago still stings to this day. A comment putting down your appearance, your intelligence, or your ability simply hurts. The more you look up to the person who said it, the louder the voice is in your mind.

Distractions.

This paragraph right here. The one you're reading now. I was stuck writing this (rather, *not* writing this) for over a week. My breakthrough came on a flight while I was playing some time-waster game on my phone. God helped me to feel very discontent about the way I was spending my time. I looked around and saw dozens of other passengers entertaining themselves on various devices. Input was everywhere. Music, movies, books. Here I had two hours to think and pray about what to write in this section, and I was choosing to distract myself with some weird version of Sudoku I'm still not sure how to play. I was convicted with the reality I cannot be entertained and be listening at the same time. If I needed to listen, I first needed to put down the distractions. I'm probably not alone in this.

Doubts.

Deceit comes from the enemy. Discouragements come from others. Distractions come from our environment. Doubts, though, are your voice in your head that can cripple good intentions before they even get off the ground. Doubts are like pet lies. You bought them; you keep them around; you give them attention; you help them grow. They get in your way when you try to walk; they pee all over your carpet . . . I mean, your metaphorical carpet. Well, you get what I'm saying. Doubt gets its material from deceit and discouragement, and when you grant those attitudes airtime, they find a home in your mind.

Remember, you can control the volume of the input. You amplify these negative voices when you choose to focus on them. To diminish them, you'll need to clear the mechanism and amplify one particular source. *The* Source. Your Creator who knows you best and wants to take care of you.

Listen up, sheeple!

Jesus says in John 10:27, "My sheep listen to my voice; I know them, and they follow me." My personal experience with sheep is pretty much limited to getting bitten at the petting zoo. So, armchair research scientist I am, I browsed YouTube and spent an inordinate amount of time watching sheep videos. You can, too, if you'd like, but allow me to spare you the time.

Sheep aren't very bright. They will walk into holes, they will repeatedly get their heads stuck in fences, they will eat too much food if it's available. The list of evidence for questionable intelligence goes on, but there seems to be one thing sheep do well: they know and respond to the voice of their shepherd. When a stranger calls out to the herd, the complete lack of response by the sheep makes it look like the stranger might as well not be saying anything. When the shepherd steps up to the fence and calls out over the pasture, however, ears twitch. Heads turn. Soon the entire flock comes bounding toward their shepherd.

Our safety, our growth, and our help come from knowing our Shepherd's voice and responding to it. But Jesus doesn't typically call out to us with a rich, booming, James Earl Jones-style voice. Most often, the voice of our Shepherd is a whisper.

A still, small voice.

The prophet Elijah had witnessed God perform one of the most dazzling, dramatic displays of his power mankind had ever seen. Elijah initiated a showdown between his God and the false god Baal. Two teams, two altars. First deity to light the altar with fire from heaven wins. Elijah gave Baal's team a head start. They hit themselves, they danced around, Elijah shot off some toilet humor; it was an entertaining time. When enough was enough, Elijah prayed to God (after making it "harder" for God by drenching His altar with water), and God launched a torrent of fire from heaven that completely consumed the altar.

You'd think this event would have propelled Elijah's faith so he would never again doubt God's ability. Think again. After the defeat of Baal's prophets, their queen vowed to see Elijah dead within twenty-four hours. This sent Elijah into a tailspin, to the point where he wanted God to kill him and end everything before it got worse. So, God called class into session.

"'Go out and stand before me on the mountain,' the Lord told him. And as Elijah stood there, the Lord passed by, and a mighty windstorm hit the mountain. It was such a terrible blast that the rocks were torn loose, but the Lord was not in the wind. After the wind there was an earthquake, but the Lord was not in the earthquake. And after the earthquake there was a fire, but the Lord was not in the fire. And after the fire there was the sound of a gentle whisper" (1 Kings 19:11-12).

The Lord was not in the wind, the earthquake, or the fire. Those were not God's attempts at communication. Those were only events.

Events in our lives can be loud and disruptive like a windstorm. They can shake us and rearrange our reality like an earthquake. Or they can cause destruction like a fire. But they're merely events. God is not likely *in* them. Where is God? He's closer than you think. And He's whispering, inviting you to lean in close.

———⁂———

I had a teacher in school who, when we were being too loud and lost in our conversations, would never raise her voice to get us to shut up. Instead, she whispered. It was drowned out by our continued clamor at first, but one by one, we heard the whisper. We leaned in. We couldn't make out what it was saying; we only knew it was there. And as more of my classmates realized she was whispering, the conversations settled down until her whispering voice was the loudest in the room.

God, like my teacher, could yell to get our attention, and we would probably respond. When the fire alarm blares, we jump up and high-tail it toward the nearest exit. But God doesn't want us to respond out of fear and intimidation or when we don't seem to have a choice.

When God whispers, He is inviting you into a relationship. His whisper requires us to lean in, tune in, and take in.

Lean in . . . by adopting a posture of readiness.

Tune in . . . by filtering out voices not from God.

Take in . . . by capturing His words and keeping them in our hearts.

This process builds up our sensitivity to the voice of our Shepherd, so we don't have to wonder if it's really Him. We can know. And when we know His voice, we can find all the peace, comfort, wisdom, and instruction He has in store for those who grow in a relationship with Him. Listening to our Shepherd is what we were created to do.

Listen to advice and accept discipline, and at the end you will be counted among the wise. Many are the plans in a person's heart, but it is the Lord's purpose that prevails. (Proverbs 19:20-21, NIV)

*** COMMERCIAL BREAK ***

We interrupt your program to bring you this exciting offer!

Do you think you're a bad listener? Do you want to *know*, beyond a shadow of a doubt, you are a bad listener? Well, for you, I have a revolutionary line of products I guarantee will help you become a definite, without-a-doubt, *bad* listener! Introducing . . .

The Bad Listener's Toolkit!

Inside you'll find . . .

Doing most of the talking!

Nothing blocks the intake of understanding more than being the primary talker in a conversation! But don't simply talk 100% of the time about whatever nonsense comes to mind, or else you'll lose your audience. Instead, master the art of interruption. Listen only enough to pick up keywords that can trigger a new topic relating to you. But for you less-talkative types, try this . . .

Doing none of the talking!

Nine out of ten bad listeners recommend this simple method! This system uses secret patented technology that makes it *look* like you are listening intently, all the while allowing you to be lost in your thoughts. Order now, and you'll receive a bonus Nod and three *Mm-hmm*'s to enhance the illusion of listening!

Not asking questions!

Are you understanding what people's opinions, concerns, or instructions are? Want to stop? Then stop asking questions! Questions are the gateway to understanding, and a true Bad Listener will stay far from them.

If you're not willing to give up question-asking cold turkey, then you might be interested in what we call *close-ended questions*. Try asking questions that can be answered in only one word, such as "yes" or "no." Never learn from a question again!

Multitasking!

Are you frustrated by how you can never get anything done while having a conversation with somebody? Introducing Multitasking! Now, you can work on the computer, do dishes, cook meals, or browse the internet on your phone—all while making it look like you are listening! The secret is, you're not "multitasking" at all! You're simply prioritizing something else over the present conversation. Order now, and we'll send you a shiny new "It's okay, I'm a good multitasker!" badge for you to wear proudly to remind the speaker that they are, in fact, being heard.

All these products can be yours today! You'll never have to worry about listening and understanding again!

*** BACK TO THE PROGRAM ***

CHAPTER 5
YES!

The Power of Agreement

Let's take a look at an improv scene starring Yessica and Nolan, two very real improv actors whose names are absolutely not made up for illustrative purposes.

Ladies and gentlemen, who's ready for some improv!?
   Alright, I need a suggestion of any type of vehicle. Yes sir, in the back? Submarine? Ah, nice. So, this next scene will have something to do with a submarine. Action!

Yessica: "Ensign, take a sonar reading. Let's see what's out there."

Nolan: "I'm not an ensign! I'm the captain!"
Yessica: "... A mutiny?"
Nolan: "And this isn't a submarine! This is a plane, and I want you to go serve snacks!"
Yessica: "Um..."

End scene!

Well, that didn't last long, did it? Did you see what happened? Nolan rejected being called the ensign in this scene. This is called denial, and it's a big no-no in improv world. Denial is, in fact, saying no to what is true. In improv, if someone says it, it's true. Nolan denied what Yessica established, and even denied the suggestion of "submarine" given in the first place. Don't be like Nolan—on stage, or in life.

Instead, adopt an attitude of Yes. I'm not talking about becoming like a 2008 romantic comedy yes-man character who agrees to do anything for anyone. What I *am* saying is the unexpected will be easier to handle when you consider God as your scene partner, and practice this attitude of yes, or acceptance, with Him. What He says is true, and the context you find yourself in is true. If you struggle with change, it's likely because you say no and buck against what has already been established as true. If you keep saying no, you're not actually making any progress forward.

Saying no is natural. We don't have to be taught it. Early in life it becomes one of our first words and one of our favorites.

"Hey Mikey, come back to the table, please."

"No!"

"Mikey, it's time to take a bath."

"No!"

"Mikey, get your teddy and go to bed."

"No! Mom! I'm thirty-three! Stop telling me what to do!"

Gee whiz. Classic parents, am I right?

The allure of the word no is the same whether we're two or thirty-two. Saying no inflates us with a sense of power and independence. Those are not inherently bad things. We do have the power to decide for ourselves, and we can exert free will. There are certainly things and people we should say no to. The trouble is when we say no to the wrong things, like situations we can't control, and God's attempts to communicate with us. In those situations, no is an expression of our pride, fear, or stubbornness.

An improviser, on the other hand, must come into every scene with an attitude of humility, trust, and willingness.

Humility in laying aside your ideas and accepting others'.

Trust in the other players who are also working for the good of the scene.

Willingness to do whatever is asked of you.

Whether your scene is a pretend submarine on stage or in a very real, difficult stage of life, *yes* is a discipline that can feel a bit forced and unnatural at first. Humility is uncomfortable. Trust is scary. Willingness is uncertain. But over time, as *yes* becomes your default response, those qualities manifest themselves more in your life.

Yes, Let's!

Whenever I train a group of people in improv, whether they are aspiring actors or corporate employees, I start the session with a game called Yes, Let's!

The rules are simple: At any time, someone in the group can suggest an activity. "Let's . . . go to the beach!" And then, the entire group must reply with the words, "Yes, let's!" and proceed to act out that activity for a few seconds until someone else suggests another activity.

The reason I love this simple game is it builds a reflex of agreement and willingness. When the first couple of activities are suggested, there are usually some eye rolls from people who for whatever reason don't want to act them out. They think they would look strange or uncomfortable if they played along. They soon realize the game goes on with or without them and failing to accept the reality of what's going on around them is actually more uncomfortable.

And so, my friend, the game is going on with or without you. But you don't have to be alone. Every involuntary change of plans, every unexpected bit of news, every interruption is God suggesting "Let's . . . walk through this together!" "Let's . . . show my love to this person!" "Let's . . . allow the Holy Spirit make you more like Jesus!"

You can respond "Yes, let's!" (it's okay if you're nervous!), or you can stand off to the side and refuse to participate. The choice is yours, but the outcomes are life-changing.

Yes is a Choice.

Have you ever played that trust-building game where you are blindfolded to navigate an obstacle course by listening to the instructions given to you by your partner?

What are the keys to success in that game? Listening, of course; we discussed that in the last chapter. You need to ignore the instructions of other competitors and the cheers of the crowd and focus on your partner. But what else? It's trust, demonstrated by agreeing with what your partner asks you to do.

How foolish you would look if your partner, who could see the entire course, told you to step up and over the cone in front of you, and you shouted back, "I don't think there's a cone there! Let me keep walking!" It wouldn't be long before you trip and fall on your face, and your video is seen by 1.2 million people on the internet.

But isn't that what we do when we ignore or avoid God's instructions? It's not like God is on a power-trip, having us dance like monkeys on a whim because He can. And He's not asking us to obey Him, all the while looming overhead with a wooden paddle to punish us if we disobey. God is simply overlooking the entire course and guiding us through the minefield of this world, closer and closer to Himself. His instructions are guardrails for how life works best. Saying no to God is really saying yes to painful consequences, wasted efforts, and lack of fulfillment. So, developing an attitude of yes with God is the most efficient way to navigate this unscripted life.

Can we take a moment to acknowledge our *choice* to say yes or no to God is a huge shout out to His love? He doesn't make us do or say anything against our will. Consequently, we can choose to disobey Him or choose not to serve Him with our lives. Those decisions break His heart, but He must still think the risk is worth it.

> **Saying no to God is really saying yes to painful consequences, wasted efforts, and lack of fulfillment.**

Yes is an Action.

So, what does saying *yes* to God actually look like? If you're like me and went to church youth group around 2001, then you probably remember singing about trading your sorrows and a seemingly endless bridge of "Yes, Lord, yes, Lord. Yes, yes, Lord. Yes, Lord, yes, Lord. Yes, yes, Lord. Yes, Lord, yes, Lord. Yes, yes, Lord. Amen!" None of us was even sure what we were agreeing to, but it was catchy.

But there's got to be more to saying yes to God than simply, well, saying yes, right?

Jesus posed this question to a group of religious leaders, in the form of a story: "A man with two sons told the older boy, 'Son, go out and work in the vineyard today.' The son answered, 'No, I won't go,' but later he changed his mind and went anyway. Then the father told the other son, 'You go,' and he said, 'Yes, sir, I will.' But he didn't go" (Matthew 21:28-30).

Which of the two sons obeyed his father? It's not the one who *said* yes; it's the one who *did* yes. *Yes* is an action. *Yes* is not idle agreement or a nod of approval. *Yes* is a put-your-money-where-your-mouth-is, get-your-butt-off-the-couch-and-do-it, leave-your-nets-at-once kind of action.

> One day as Jesus was walking along the shore of the Sea of Galilee, he saw two brothers—Simon, also called Peter, and Andrew—throwing a net into the water, for they fished for a living.* Jesus called out to them, "Come, follow me, and I will show you how to fish for people!" And they left their nets at once and followed him. A little farther up the shore he saw two other brothers, James and John, sitting in a boat with their father, Zebedee, repairing their nets. And he called them to come, too. They immediately followed him, leaving the boat and their father behind. (Matthew 4:18-22)

In Jesus' day, Jewish teachers would invite students to be their disciples. The disciples would follow the teacher, or rabbi, around and soak up all the wisdom they could. Naturally, the rabbis would recruit the most promising, well-read students from the steps of the temple. So, the fact that Jesus

---

* Matthew clarifies the reason for the net-throwing, in case you thought they were just random net-throwers, apparently. Thanks, Matt.

called and led disciples was not unusual. What *was* unusual was He went to the beach and called some callous-handed, mollusk-scented, synagogue drop-outs to quit their full-time job and follow Him. And they did! On the spot. It had been years since they gave up wanting to be a rabbi's prized pupil. As far as they were concerned, they would be fishermen until the day they died. But Jesus came along with an invitation to refocus their calling. It would change their lives. They knew that. What they didn't know was their yes would go on to change the world.

About thirty years prior, one of the most unexpected, unbelievable turn of events in history happened to a teenage girl named Mary. After an angel dropped by for a surprise visit and unloaded the truth that she would be the mother of the Savior of the world, she responded, "I am the Lord's servant. May everything you have said about me come true" (Luke 1:38).

Later, Mary was filled with a song recorded for all of history, with the very Broadway-musical-sounding name of *Magnificat.* I seriously love how the New King James Version puts it: "My soul magnifies the Lord!" (Luke 1:46, NKJV). What an amazing attitude of *yes* to God! Mary was basically saying, "Every part of me wants You and Your plan to flourish."

It would be a sacrifice. Her reputation would be questioned almost immediately. Others would not be able to understand or relate to her. And her heart would break. This turn of events changed her life forever, but she aligned her desires with those of God, and in so doing magnified the Lord.

You will never be given quite the same responsibility God gave Mary. But God offers other responsibilities and opportunities that often come in the form of a major interruption and they may require sacrifices. In those moments, you will respond in your soul. You may resist and fight, and try to continue on your way, or your soul may magnify the Lord.

You're not going to get it right every time. I know I don't. Fortunately, God gives us countless opportunities to respond with yes to Him. Each time we do, we become more familiar with His voice and more trusting of His goodness. This process of acceptance—aligning our will with the will of God—is how we become more like Jesus. Jesus, in a moment of extreme anguish before his death, prayed this:

"Father, if you are willing, please take this cup of suffering away from me. Yet I want your will to be done, not mine" (Luke 22:42).

Jesus set the standard of *yes* we are to follow. That simple prayer offers a great model of how we should say yes to God: Recognize your relationship, request your ideal, and relinquish your will.

> This process of acceptance—aligning our will with the will of God—is how we become more like Jesus.

Recognize your relationship.

In this time of emotional turmoil, Jesus went straight to His Father. Although Jesus did invite

His friends to come pray with Him in this scenario, they fell asleep and didn't offer much support. There's value in close friendships through hard times, but they cannot be the source of your encouragement and strength. They will fail you and disappoint you sometimes. But God never sleeps, never tires of your same prayers, and is a Rock in times of trouble. He goes by "Father," because He is everything you expect a good father to be and more. No other god I know of in the history of religion invites you to call him by such a close relational name. Recognize the relationship and lean on your Father.

Request your ideal.

Jesus didn't shy away from the fact that He really, *really* did not want to go through with the emotional and physical pain of what was coming. So, He straight-up asked God to make it all stop. But it was with an attitude of humility and prefaced with, *if you are willing*.

"If it's okay with you, God, could you please find another way? I understand if you decide not to, but honestly, I'm struggling with this."

What amazing transparency Jesus allows us to witness! He requested His ideal. But He understood His human ideal was not necessarily His Father's ideal.

Relinquish your will.

And so, Jesus relinquished His right to fight for His plan. "I want your will to be done, not mine."

Does that seem weak to you? I'm asking honestly. Does that seem like a weak thing to say? I ask because in my life, when I have adopted such a posture with other people, it looks more like "Never mind what I want. It doesn't matter. Whatever you want is fine." The phrase "relinquish your will" isn't particularly popular in today's empowerment culture, and it might not sit well with you. If so, track with me for a minute.

My family visited a Budweiser plant (topic shift, I know, but keep tracking with me). Whether or not you've visited a plant, you are probably familiar with the signature Clydesdale horses Budweiser uses to pull their beer wagons around events. If you haven't seen them in person before, let me tell you: they are *big*. Not like horses are big. No. Like, this beast could step on me and kick me into oblivion and not even notice. If the Clydesdales wanted to, they could kick down the fence and abscond with the entire beer wagon and there would be nothing anybody could do about it. But they don't. These enormously powerful beasts have, for whatever reason, allowed us puny humans to tie ropes to them, attach wagons to them, and even braid their hair! Does this make them less powerful? No! They retain their strength, but they relinquish their will. There's a simple word for this: meekness. Meek does not equal weak. Weakness is losing your will. Meekness means choosing to set it aside.

Jesus personified meekness when He allowed Himself to be captured and killed. When He was being arrested, He told His terrified disciples, "Don't you realize that I could ask my Father for thousands of angels to protect us, and he would send them instantly? But if I did, how would the Scriptures be fulfilled that describe what must happen now?" (Matthew 26: 53-54). With the power of thousands of angels at His command, Jesus relinquished His will. "I want your will to be done, not mine."

Recognize your relationship, request your ideal, and relinquish your will. This is the model of how we say yes to our God who knows the big picture and is ultimately fighting for our best interests, which is to be like Jesus. And in this process, God sometimes says no to what we want. But contrary to what many people think, God is not a God of no.

God's Ultimate Yes.

The apostle Paul had a special relationship with the church in Corinth. He personally helped the Corinthian church get started. He knew the names of all the greeters at the door; he raved about the casserole Achaius' wife always brought to the potluck; he knew where they kept extra coffee stirrers if the welcome center ran out. In one letter he wrote to the Corinthians, he said,

> I am coming to visit you after I have been to Macedonia, for I am planning to travel

through Macedonia. Perhaps I will stay awhile with you, possibly all winter, and then you can send me on my way to my next destination. This time I don't want to make just a short visit and then go right on. I want to come and stay awhile, if the Lord will let me. (1 Corinthians 16:5-7)

Well, guess what? Paul never showed up. And apparently, the Corinthians were starting to murmur and question the integrity of Paul's word. "Maybe he only said that to make us happy? Maybe he's spending time with another church instead? Maybe he likes the potlucks in Ephesus better?"

Paul heard about the church's grumblings and wrote a second letter. He gave his greetings, yadda yadda yadda, and then jumped right to the point:

You may be asking why I changed my plan. Do you think I make my plans carelessly? Do you think I am like people of the world who say "Yes" when they really mean "No"? As surely as God is faithful, our word to you does not waver between "Yes" and "No." For Jesus Christ, the Son of God, does not waver between "Yes" and "No." He is the one whom Silas, Timothy, and I preached to you, and *as God's ultimate "Yes,"* he always does what he says. For all of God's promises have been fulfilled in Christ with a resounding "Yes!" And through Christ, our "Amen" (which means "Yes") ascends to God for his glory. (2 Cor. 1:17–20, emphasis mine)

God Himself models an attitude of *yes* through the sending of His Son, Jesus. Jesus is the *yes* to all of God's promises—everything your heart aches for in this world. God is for you! He's on your side. Satan will try to convince you disappointments and heartbreak mean God is against you and doesn't care. But God has already said yes to the things your soul craves. *Does my life have purpose?* Yes! *Is there hope?* Absolutely! *Does anyone love me?* More than you can possibly know.

"What shall we say about such wonderful things as these? If God is for us, who can ever be against us? Since he did not spare even his own Son but gave him up for us all, won't he also give us everything else?" (Romans 8:31-32)

How unfortunate it is that Christians are often thought of as the group that says no. *Can I do this?* No. *Can I drink this?* No. *Do I belong here?* No. When Christians are the first and loudest to say no, people who are looking for hope end up finding a Christ who has apparently rejected them.

If you are a Christian, you have already accepted God's ultimate yes. Now it's your job to maintain an attitude of yes—obedience to the mission God has for you. The mission is to share God's ultimate yes with those around you, believers or not. Assure them God is for them. For their restoration. For their joy. For their peace. For their reconciliation with God and others.

CHAPTER 6

AND!

The Virtue of Adding Value

In improv, it's not enough merely to agree.

"Hi, I'm the new salesman. You must be my supervisor."

"Yes, I am."

"Great! Is . . .this my desk?"

"Yes, it is."

"Okay . . . I think I need some coffee first. Can I get you some?"

"Yes."

"Sugar or cream?"

"Yes."

"Um, okay. Coming right up. Where's the coffee maker?"

"Yes."

End scene!

This scene kept going, for the most part. I mean, it didn't crash and burn like our scene with Nolan last chapter (thanks a lot, Nolan), but it grew at half speed. The "supervisor" only agreed with what was being said and done. He didn't contribute any information or value to the scene, which put the other actor in the position of having to come up with the next line.

Here's the same scene, after I had a stern, finger-wagging talking-to with the supervisor about this problem. It should be better now.

"Hi, I'm the new salesman. Are you my supervisor?"

"Yes, I am! Here's your desk. Sorry about the coffee stain on the chair."

"Oh! That's okay. It does remind me I haven't had my coffee yet, though. Can I get you some, too?"

"Yes. Sugar and cream."

"Coming right up!"

"Coffee machine's the other direction."

"Oh! Thanks! Be back in a jiffy!"

"He'll never last . . ."

When both actors *listen* to each other, agree to *agree*, and *add* to what the other person said, you end up with a rich and interesting scene. That's why *yes* is only useful when it's followed by *and*. Together, they form the mantra of improvisers across the world—*"Yes, and!"* Maybe you've heard it before?

It's important to note you don't have to literally say the two words together to show you are agreeing and adding to the scene. As with *yes* in the previous chapter, *and* is an attitude. It's an attitude eager to add value to another person, regardless of the circumstances. And now—you guessed it—we're talking about real life again.

Are you a fountain or a drain?

There are two types of people: Fountain people, Drain people, and those who can't count. But I'm going to focus on the Fountains and the Drains.

Fountains are those who add value to others. After an encounter with a Fountain, people leave feeling fuller than before the interaction. As Christians, we are called to be Fountains.

"Above all, love each other deeply, because love covers over a multitude of sins. Offer hospitality to one another without grumbling. Each of you should use whatever gift you have received to serve others, as faithful stewards of God's grace in its various forms" (1 Peter 4:8-10, NIV).

Check out those verbs. Love, offer, and serve. *Love*, because relationships should come first. *Offer*, and without grumbling, because our attitude reveals our hearts. And *serve*, because we have been freely given so much. Can't you feel the bubbly, fountain-y action of these words?

Drains, on the other hand, are consumers of the value offered by Fountains. They take without adding value to anyone else. They force the

Fountains to carry the burden with their creativity, resources, and energy. Not to mention the clumps of hair and toothpaste they collect.

Paul was determined to not be a Drain when he was visiting the church in Corinth. "And when I was with you and didn't have enough to live on, I did not become a financial burden to anyone. For the brothers who came from Macedonia brought me all that I needed. I have never been a burden to you, and I never will be" (2 Corinthians 11:9).

And again, with the church in Thessalonica. "Don't you remember, dear brothers and sisters, how hard we worked among you? Night and day, we toiled to earn a living so that we would not be a burden to any of you as we preached God's Good News to you" (1 Thessalonians 2:9).

So, the next logical question is: are you a Fountain or a Drain? You're probably not one or the other all the time. I know as often as I try to be a Fountain, there are times when I'm tired, overwhelmed, or sick (as my wife will attest), and I get focused on myself and my circumstances.

When circumstances change unexpectedly, it's difficult to remain a Fountain. But in these times, people aren't *expecting* you to add value and take a stance of love, offering, and service. So when you do, it has a greater impact.

Well, of course, Mike. It's not like I don't want *to be that kind of person.*

Right on. Okay, so if you want to be a person who adds value, even in tough times, you need to know and believe two important things:

- You can only add value when you *see* value.
- You can only add value when you *have* value.

Seeing Value.

When Jesus was on earth, He put on a masterclass in seeing value in people. Literally. Once, He and His disciples were doing some people-watching at the collection box at the temple. Rich people were putting on a pretty public display of how much money they were donating. They were making it rain denarii! Other people would watch, applaud, and think, *Wow! Maybe I could be rich like that some day! Then imagine how much God would appreciate me!*

The disciples were so transfixed on the rich people dumping out their pockets full of coins onto the stone floor that Jesus had to call them over to notice someone everybody else had missed. One poor widow, head down, reached over to the collection box. "Plink. Plink." (She didn't *say* "plink, plink." That was the sound of coins dropping . . . anyway). She gave her two cents, then Jesus gave His.

"I tell you the truth," (Jesus' way of saying *believe it or not*) "this poor widow has given more than all the others who are making contributions. For they gave a tiny part of their surplus, but she, poor as she is, has given everything she had to live on" (Mark 12:43-44).

This woman was not considered to be of much value in her day. She was a woman, which unfortunately was not valued as highly in her culture at the time. Furthermore, she was a widow, and therefore dependent on the rare generosity of strangers for survival. Isn't it interesting she's the one who saw value in her God and wanted to add value by giving one hundred percent to Him? And she didn't care if anybody saw. In fact, she hoped no one would.

But Jesus saw this woman, saw great value, and wanted her to be the example His disciples would remember and record for us to read about today.

If we want to add value, we need to be able to see value in others. And if we want to see value in others, we need to change how we look at people. By all outward appearances in her day, this widow had no value. But, "the Lord does not look at the things people look at. People look at the outward appearance, but the Lord looks at the heart" (1 Samuel 16:7).

And when we look at someone's heart—their attitudes, their intentions—can I be honest? It's *still* sometimes difficult to see value in people. Especially people whose hearts are not healthy spiritually. In these cases, I need to fall back on the realization that while we were *still sinners*, Jesus died for us (Romans 5:8). God saw the value in us before we could even hope to have our act together. We can do the same for others.

Having Value.

But you can't be a Fountain if you're a dry well. In order to add value, you obviously have to possess it in the first place.

Can I pause here a moment to tell you, my friend, in case you are still struggling with the concept . . . *you have incredible value!* You don't have to take my word when Jesus Himself says it:

"What is the price of two sparrows—one copper coin? But not a single sparrow can fall to the ground without your Father knowing it. And the very hairs on your head are all numbered. So, don't be afraid; you are more valuable to God than a whole flock of sparrows" (Matthew 10:29-31).

You might be trying to do the math. *Two sparrows for a penny. Maybe four or five hundred sparrows in a flock? So, I'm worth at least . . . two bucks? And some quarters?*

Try again. Peter ups the ante when he reminds us God paid the ransom to save us from our hopeless life. Not with mere gold or silver, but with the death of His perfect son (1 Peter 1:18-19). That's how valuable you are. Don't let anyone try to convince you that you are worth anything less. Got it?

Okay. So, we agree you have value that can never be taken away. But when it comes to being a Fountain, you can get drained. And like any fountain, if you aren't connected to the source, you won't have anything to offer anybody.

The metaphor was certainly not lost on Jesus. Jesus, in a teaching moment by an actual well, called Himself living water (John 4). Another time, He likened Himself to a vine (John 15). We, the branches, need to be attached to the Vine in order to produce any good thing.

If we want any chance of adding value to people in the most draining of circumstances, we must have what we give. But

Jesus promises to refill whatever we pour out.

we cannot be our source. Living out *and* requires a constant relationship with Jesus, who promises to refill whatever we pour out.

And What?

But what do we pour out? We know when the unexpected happens, we should lean in and listen for God's voice, yield our will to His in an attitude of *yes*, and add value to the people involved. But what value do we have to add?

Add your experience.

Have you wondered why God doesn't simply take away the pain and trouble we experience? That's a lot to unpack, but I can point you to this verse: "God is our merciful Father and the source of all comfort. He comforts us in all our troubles so that we can comfort others. When they are troubled, we will be able to give them the same comfort God has given us" (2 Corinthians 1:3-4).

God is the source of all comfort. When we draw from that source, His comfort is not only enough to help us through our difficulties in the moment, but also to keep in our pocket to share with others down the road. God doesn't waste a single tear, and He redeems every unexpected struggle in our life. Each experience can be used for the building up of ourselves and others.

Add your gifts.

"A spiritual gift is given to each of us so we can help each other" (1 Corinthians 12:7). God has empowered His team of believers with abilities like the X-Men. Except, instead of being able to turn blue and spiky, we can give wise advice. And instead of laser eyes, we can have discernment. So, maybe not blockbuster movie material, but our gifts are very real and powerful. And, like the X-Men, our gifts work best when we work as a team and for the benefit of others.

Discovering your spiritual gift is one of the most important early missions you have as a Christian. If you don't already know, talk to your pastor or mentor to help. Chances are, other people have felt the effects of your gift already, and you only need to be aware of it and become intentional.

Add your effort.

Paul, who we've already established as a champion of good old fashioned elbow-grease, wrote in his letter to the church in Ephesus, "Use your hands for good hard work, and then give generously to others in need" (Ephesians 4:28).

Paul even put an "and" in there to help me out in this chapter. Thanks, Paul! So, he's saying work hard [to avoid being a drain], *AND* then give generously [to be a fountain].

God of And.

This idea of generosity is the driving force behind a life of *and*. On the improv stage, adding value through details and ideas is considered a gift. A generous improviser is one who is a fountain of creativity. To be an improviser in real life, it's not about rolling with the punches. It's about going a step beyond to give to others and give back to God. When we are generous, we are modeling the character of God Himself. He has been *and*-ing us for ages.

The word *and* appears over 60,000 times in the Bible. For the rest of this chapter, let's go through each of these instances together.

No? Okay fine, on your time then. Instead, how about this one instance? If there was ever any question about why Jesus came to earth, He spelled it out for us in John 10:10. I like how the NIV phrases it. "I have come that they may have life and have it to the full."

Have life and have it to the full! But how often do we live like He said, "I have come that they may have life, and . . . they'll be miserable, but at least they're not dead, so they better be thankful"? No! He came so we could live, *and* live in an abundance of love *and* joy *and* peace. Now that's a lot of *and*.

And… what's next?

If you listen and adhere to *Yes, And* in improv, you'll do well. Likewise, in this unscripted life, if you listen to God's whisper, accept His will, and add value to others, you'll do well, too. But in both cases, there are more tips and tricks to have life and live it to the full. Each chapter from now on will dig into a different role Jesus played as the Master Improviser we talked about in Chapter 2 and explore the parallels with some of the more advanced principles of improv.

PART THREE
THRIVING ON THE STAGE OF LIFE

CHAPTER 7

GIVE UP!

Be a Relationship-Builder

In the movie *Don't Think Twice*, we follow the story of an improv troupe in New York City. They had all the chemistry, wit, and camaraderie you could hope to see in an improv team. After each crowd-pleasing performance, they would unwind at the bar and dream about the day they would "make it big."

The night a talent scout from a national sketch comedy program attended their show, the dream suddenly seemed within reach. The show started strong, the troupe energized by the challenge and excitement of the scout's presence in the audience. But ambition got the better of one actor, who stepped forward to deliver a monologue in his Barack Obama impression. After he stole the show with several other characters and impressions, his teammates were furious. As hard as he tried to justify his choices, there was no getting around the fact he was showboating in an attempt to get noticed.

It only made matters worse when he *did* get noticed and offered a role on television. His promotion left a wake of disappointment, betrayal, and bitterness in his group of former friends. This interaction reminds me of a conversation in Mark 10, when two of Jesus' disciples, James and John, went to Jesus and said something like, "Hey, so you know how you're gonna have a kingdom?"

"Yeah."

"So, you're gonna be like a king, right?"

"Yeah."

"So, when you're the king, can we be your number one and number two guys? You can pick who's one and who's two, but can we sit next to your throne and stuff?"

The other disciples heard about their request and were furious. We can relate, can't we?

There's something about someone pursuing selfish gain that rubs us the wrong way. Not only because we have this innate sense that people ought not to be selfish, but if we're honest, also because we wish we could get the promotion, too.

That's why Jesus took this as a teaching moment with His disciples.

"Whoever wants to be a leader among you must be your servant, and whoever wants to be

first among you must be the slave of everyone else"
(Mark 10:43-44).

Be careful not to glaze over that sentence. *Yeah,
yeah. First shall be last, last shall be first. Heard it. Got
it.* No, for real; think about it! In this unscripted
life, there will come moments when you have a
choice to make. Will you put yourself first? Or
will you put others first? If you continually look
out only for your interests, you'll eventually find
yourself alone and lacking anything of value. Serve
others, though, Jesus says, and not only will you
be successfully navigating this life, but you will be
leading others to do the same.

This mentality of putting the group ahead of
self comes second-nature to experienced improvisers on stage. How much more should it describe
us as Christians?

Chivalry Isn't Dead!

In improv, this servant's mindset is called "chivalry." Thus, behold! Presenting . . .
   Ye Olde Rules of Chivalrous Behavior!

- Make each other look good.
- Don't highlight mistakes.
- Consider others better than yourself.
- Share the load.
- Don't be afraid to get messy.

If you follow these rules on stage, your fellow
improvisers will want to work with you in every
scene you do. And of course, if you follow these

rules in life, your presence on any team will be in high demand.

Make each other look good.

My favorite moments on stage with 321 Improv typically involve the game Party Quirks. Jeremy and I have the benefit of knowing what each other's characters are, while Carl must figure us out through our crazy interactions. Jeremy is an expert in finding connections and setting others up for the punchline. When he was a "foot-smeller" and I was "afraid of the floor," he got down on his hands and knees to sniff at Carl's feet. What he was secretly doing, though, was offering me a way to get around without touching the floor. So, I sat on his back and held my foot out in front of his face like putting a carrot in front of a donkey. That synergy looked like my bright idea, but in reality, it was only due to Jeremy setting me up. It then became my goal to find opportunities to set him up for clever moments later.

Making others look good requires you to:

- **Give up** your right to take credit.
- **Set up** for their success.
- **Stand up** for what they decide.

You have the power to make others look like geniuses or to make them look like idiots. What you do and say *to* a person are powerful; what you show and say to others *about* them is more powerful. Making others look good is a public thing. We can also call it "honor."

Romans 12:10 tells us to "Take delight in honoring each other." In other words, make others look good, and have fun doing it!

Don't highlight mistakes.

You want to know what kills honor faster than it can get built?

"I'm guessing, by the title of this section, the answer is *highlighting mistakes*?"

Oh. Yeah. Forgot about that. Good eye. But yes, highlighting mistakes. Anyway, I can't tell you how many times on stage I've had a line fall flat, a sentence get jumbled, or an accent shift from Russian to Irish-Pirate-Texan. Now, I usually can't escape ridicule for the last one, but here's the point: When you highlight someone's mistakes (bringing others' attention to them), it has multiple negative effects.

- They don't feel safe to try things.
- They don't feel respected by their peers.
- They focus on their mistakes instead of successes.

Paul begged the Christians in Ephesus to "always be humble and gentle. Be patient with each other, making allowance for each other's faults because of your love" (Ephesians 4:2).

Be humble, gentle, and patient. Allow a margin of error. Why? Because we lower our expectations of excellence? Because the task isn't important? No. Because of your love. Love defends publicly. Love doesn't mean we have to ignore completely whenever anybody does something wrong. Because love also corrects privately. But if we view a person through the lens of how much God loves them, I think we'll realize grace finds far less fault than we do.

> If we view a person through the lens of how much God loves them, I think we'll realize grace finds far less fault than we do.

Consider others better than yourself.

If you struggle with wanting to make others look good and not pointing out their faults, it may be because, at some level, you consider yourself better than them. Can we be honest for a minute here? Take a regrettable peek inside my brain.

"He shouldn't get the credit; *I'm* the one who had the idea!"

"If *I* were in charge, I wouldn't have made that mistake."

I've actually thought these things! And 100% of the time, it's because I considered myself to be the more creative one, the more thoughtful one, the more (dare I say it) humble one.

"Don't be selfish; don't try to impress others. Be humble, thinking of others as better than yourselves" (Philippians 2:3).

Please don't read this as another bullet point in the *do*s and *don't*s list so many people (incorrectly) consider the Bible to be. This is a heart check we need to perform, maybe even multiple times a day, so we don't let our pride and ambition get in the way of healthy, life-giving relationships with those around us.

When you find yourself judging someone and elevating yourself in your mind, ask yourself:

- What value do they offer that I can't?
- What strengths do they have?
- What have I seen them do well?

Considering others better than yourself doesn't mean you think yourself worthless, putrid trash. It doesn't mean looking at someone's glamorous social media presence and thinking their life is better than yours. It's choosing to recognize the value they add, admiring their strengths, and rejoicing in their successes.

One question my wife and I will ask each other when we're struggling with negative thoughts about someone is, "What are three things you like about them?"

At first, it seems like a shallow question deserving of an eyeroll. And often, the first answer might be a little shallow. The second answer usually comes fairly easily, too. There's something about having to list three, though, that makes you really dig down and think. The process of thinking about the positive, and the time spent thinking about someone's good points, rewires the brain away from the negativity and pride.

If you decide to think three positive things about a person for every one negative one, you'll find the negative thoughts popping up far less frequently.

Share the load.

Sharing the load in an improv scene is really two reminders in one: First, don't force the other actors to have to carry the scene (remember talking about adding value with *and*?). And second, don't carry the scene yourself.

There's an improv warm-up that still terrifies me. It's often called The Hot Spot. Actors stand in a circle and come up with a topic. Water, for example. Then, one person jumps into the middle and starts singing a song about water.

"Sittin' on the dock of the bay . . ."

They only need to sing a phrase or two. Many people can't go much further anyway. Some could go the whole song, but this isn't a solo concert, either. Regardless, by then, it's expected that someone else jumps in and rescues the person in the middle by singing another song, whether they're ready or not.

"I'm siiiiiinging in the rain. Just siiiiiiiinging in the rain!"

Sound scary? Well, like I said, it is. But it's worth it for the takeaways for the participants:

- Helping the person in The Hot Spot is more important than your comfort, and
- When you are in The Hot Spot, you can trust someone will help you out of it.

Man, in this unscripted life, we find ourselves in Hot Spots all the time, don't we? And if it's not us, it's someone we know. That's why it's so important to have your circle, people who will jump in and share the load, and who you can pull out of their Hot Spots.

"Share each other's burdens, and in this way obey the law of Christ. If you think you are too important to help someone, you are only fooling yourself. You are not that important" (Galatians 6:2-3).

Ouch. Paul's personal shot aside, the point is this: the burdens of this life are not meant to be carried alone—by you or anybody else. Share the load.

Don't be afraid to get messy.

Sometimes the burden is messy. One thing I've experienced on stage is not all roles are desirable. Some seem degrading, some are unattractive, and some are physically messy. In improv, sometimes those roles are assigned to you.

I've always admired actors who aren't afraid to get messy. Actors like Lucille Ball, Tina Fey, and Christian Bale are known for putting their A-list appearances aside for the job when it required looking less-than-put-together.

One aspect of chivalry in improv is the willingness to accept any role, regardless of how it will make you look. In sharing the load, no job is beneath you.

In Jesus' day, back when people and donkeys walked the same dusty streets, it was expected for the host of a dinner to offer to wash guests' feet. Of course, no host actually wanted to do it themselves, so they typically had a servant do it.

So, when Jesus hosted a dinner for his disciples, it didn't take long before they started whispering.

"So, uh . . . who's gonna wash our feet?"

"Good point. I mean, we can't expect Jesus to do it."

"Well, of course not. But there's no servant here."

"You do it." "Why me?"

"Your feet are the grossest. Just do it."

"No way! Have John do it. He's the youngest."

Jesus, without saying a word, took off His robe and wrapped a towel around His waist. They knew what that meant.

"Wait, Jesus—don't—"

"Shh!"

"No, we can't—"

He poured water into a bowl and began to wash and dry their feet. When He had gone all the way down the line (including, might I add, the feet of the one who would soon walk out the door to betray Him), He taught them with words and actions I'm sure stuck with them until the day they died.

"Since I, your Lord and Teacher, have washed your feet, you ought to wash each other's feet. I have given you an example to follow. Do as I have done to you" (John 13:14-15).

It was never about the task. It was about the posture. If we are unwilling to get down into the mess of people's lives and do the undesirables, then we are considering ourselves better than the King who called Himself Servant.

The One Case for Denial.

Remember when we were talking about the importance of *yes*, I said one big no-no was *denial*. While it's still true, we find the word *denial* popping up in our discussion about chivalry, giving up, and being a relationship-builder. Because when we say *yes* to God and consider His will more important than ours, it inherently requires us to deny ourselves.

Bill Hull, in *The Complete Book of Discipleship*, says, "When we follow Jesus, we deny ourselves the right to justice in human relationships. We deny ourselves the right to a good reputation and immediate vindication."[1]

When Jesus was on earth, people did not treat Him justly. He was the target of conspiracies and plots. And He withheld His right for vindication all the way to His death. Why? Because He denied himself what He deserved so He could better serve the people God loved. If we want to live a life of purpose, we should be prepared to do the same.

CHAPTER 8

BE SPECIFIC!

Be a Problem-Solver

Once upon a time, the city of Cityville was being generally bothered by the evil Dr. Vague. You see, Dr. Vague was doing stuff to people. He did something with a thing and then stuff happened. And stuff would have *kept* happening if our hero hadn't heard the people calling, "Help!"

"It's a yellow-rumped warbler! It's a Boeing 737! It's Captain Specificity!

"Greetings, citizens! What seems to be the trouble?" Captain Specificity grinned confidently, arms akimbo.

"Everything!"

"Oh my, it's worse than I thought!" Captain Specificity immediately vaulted into his midnight blue 1973 Specificity-mobile convertible and raced off to Dr. Vague's lair.

Dr. Vague was there to greet him. "Ah, yes. It's you!"

"What are you up to this time, Dr. Vague?"

"Something."

"I should have known!"

Dr. Vague remained calm. "You're too late. Just before you arrived, I pushed *this thing!*"

Captain Specificity squinted his steely blue eyes. "You mean the large red button that activates a spring-loaded trap right where you're standing?"

Right then, a spring-loaded trap activated right where Dr. Vague was standing.

"Noooo!!! Not again!"

Captain Specificity brushed the dust off his white leather gloves.

"Mission accomplished," he congratulated himself as he took a bite of the Doctor's roasted red pepper panini and returned home to his oceanside villa.

—m—

Even today, improvisers across the country are plagued by the infamous Dr. Vague. In an attempt to add value with their *and*, they make weak offerings of *I brought this!* and *Look at that!* These seem helpful at first, but in reality, they don't provide useful information.

The intent is there. An improviser who holds out his hand and says, "Look what I found in the attic!" usually has an idea in mind. *I found an old treasure map in a trunk!* But without this explanation, the scene partner feels the need to move the scene forward alone, so he responds, "Ew! A dead mouse!" And, well . . . then that's where the scene goes. Next time, the improviser will learn to be more specific.

The more specific you are, the more value you add.

I totally understand why an improviser would tend to be vague. It could be because nothing detailed comes to mind and they hope someone else can contribute, or maybe it's due to a lack of confidence in their idea.

In this unscripted life, we can resort to vague responses for the same reasons. Specifically (since it seems fitting), in the way we try to serve others, and in the way we pray. Since serving others and growing in our relationship with God is the goal of improvising our unexpected events, it's important we maximize the value in these situations. And like I said, greater specificity, greater value.

The more specific you are, the more value you add.

Specific Service

Being specific on stage does three things for the performance: it provides value others can use, it inspires other improvisers' creativity, and can help paint a more vibrant picture for the audience.

Provide value others can use.

Let me share with you the one thing I remember from physics class. Don't worry, it has nothing to do with Newton's laws or the formula for gravitational pull. There's a reason I'm doing improv now. Rather, it's a story my teacher told about walking down the road one freezing morning and passing a homeless man. He didn't want to ignore the man completely, so he smiled and introduced himself. After a short interaction, he walked away with a wave and said, "Keep warm!"

He didn't get too far before God brought to his mind a soberingly relevant Bible verse. "Suppose you see a brother or sister who has no food or clothing, and you say, 'Good-bye and have a good day; stay warm and eat well'—but then you don't give that person any food or clothing. What good does that do?" (James 2:15-16). My teacher turned around, returned to the man, and gave him the coat off his back.

A vague blessing of "Keep warm" is nothing compared to the specific blessing of "Keep my coat." In unexpected interactions, it's easy to stay vague and offer only our intentions. But remember, Jesus was a problem-solver, not merely a problem-acknowledger. Being like Jesus means offering something that can actually change someone.

Inspire other improvisers' creativity.

When a fellow improviser starts adding specific details to enrich the scene, it inspires me to step up my contributions.

After reading an earlier draft of this section, my wife said "Mike, this chapter of all places, you need to give a specific example." Fair point. So, take the example of 321 Improv's founder, Carl.

We were performing at a conference and had multiple sets throughout the day. After one such session, the group was dismissed for breakaway discussions, which left the auditorium empty. I had nothing to do but wait, so I spent my time idly. Minutes passed, and I found a funny video about a red panda to share, so I thought, "Where's Carl?"

Carl was scouring the auditorium, row by row, picking up bottles, cans, and papers left behind by the conference-goers. I bookmarked the red panda video and joined Carl, along with Jeremy, in the clean-up. Soon, some of the organizers of the event came out and found us in (and under and behind) the seats. "I knew we were hiring comedians; I didn't know we were hiring custodians, too!" And then *they* walked with us row by row until the auditorium was ready for the next session!

"Let us think of ways to motivate one another to acts of love and good works" (Hebrews 10:24). Carl took advantage of the opportunity to serve in a specific, immediate way, and it inspired others to follow suit. When those closest to us see us adding value, especially when it is our response to the unexpected, they are inspired to build on that and offer what they can provide.

Paint a more vibrant picture for the audience.

Your scene partner isn't the only one who benefits from the details you provide. The entire audience, in fact, begins to see the world you create through the details you share.

I remember talking to a woman after a show in which, at some point, I had mimed and interacted with an invisible kitchen—cabinets, refrigerator, stove, faucet, all the appliances and details I could think of as I prepared imaginary pancakes.* She came to tell me her impression of the scene. "It's like I could see what you were seeing! I could see the whole kitchen!"

I was thankful for her sharing her experience, and it showed me the importance of specific details. The more specific I was, the more I could *see*. And the more I could *see*, the clearer the picture became for those watching. Soon, they were seeing what I was.

As a follower of Jesus with a mission to help the world see Him, who calls Himself *Love*, can't we learn from this? The more specifically we love— not with intentions and well-wishes and *I'll pray for you*'s, but with actions, encouraging words, and focused prayer—the clearer God's love is for those who are watching.

---

* In many ways, my job is similar to that of a four-year-old

And trust me, they are watching. Whether it's your plan that derails or someone else's, as a Christian, your response is being watched. You have an audience. Whatever your circumstance, paint them a compelling picture of God's love in action.

Specific Prayer

Our God is a specific God, and He invites us to be specific in the way we communicate with Him.

Jesus' disciples were around for many of his prayers and sensed they were different, somehow. So, they finally asked him, "How can we pray like that?" Jesus responded with what is now one of the most famous prayers.

You're probably familiar with the line, "Give us this day our daily bread." Have you thought about how specific that is? I know; He could have specified

> God invites us to be specific in the way we communicate with Him.

pumpernickel or something, but the point isn't the bread. The point is, when we find ourselves in need and we cry out to God, we can get more specific than "I need help!" or "Please provide for me!" We can say "Father, I don't even know how I'm going to get through this day. Today, could you give me enough food (or energy, or peace, or money, or wisdom) to help through the day?

And I have to say, God isn't sitting back, waiting for us to be specific enough to enable Him to act. He's not listening to our prayer, thinking, "You need help? Well what kind of help? I can't help you until you tell me what you need! Use your words!"

Fortunately, we're told that when we are so distressed we don't even know what to pray, the Holy Spirit "prays for us with groanings that cannot be expressed in words" (Romans 8:26). So, we can trust God hears our heart even when we can't put words to it.

But in the times we *can* put two thoughts together, why are we still so hesitant to be specific with our prayers?

"God, please help me."

"God, please bless us."

Or, in the case of a blind man named Bartimaeus, "Have mercy on me!"

We find his story in Mark 10. Bartimaeus, a blind beggar stationed by the gate of a major city, heard Jesus was approaching. He called out to him, "Son of David! Have mercy on me!"

Now, "Have mercy on me," would have been a pretty standard plea for any beggar to any passer-by. But Bartimaeus was in the presence of Jesus. Did he understand what that could mean?

So, Jesus called him closer and drew out specifics. "What do you want me to do for you?"

"I want to see!"

And immediately, he could see, which Jesus credited to his faith.

Bartimaeus' daily routine was interrupted by the presence of Jesus, who came forward with an opportunity to change his entire reality. The life change hinged on Bartimaeus getting specific with his request. When you get more specific in your prayers, you will experience clarity, vulnerability, and faith that will forever change the way you walk with Jesus.

Vague vs. clear

"Mercy" could have meant anything for Bartimaeus. And, certainly, he would have accepted anything. The modern-day, cardboard-sign equivalent would say "Anything helps." Handouts of coins, scraps of food. Mercy could come in several forms, many of which could be provided by anybody. But when he approached the Son of God, Bartimaeus was invited to ask specifically for what only God could give.

When you approach the throne of God in prayer, do you ask for generic help and blessings? Or do you make your request to the God who, as Jesus reveals in Luke 12:7, knows the specific number of hairs on your head?

By asking "What do you want me to do for you?" Jesus was not asking for the sake of His clarity. He was asking so Bartimaeus could clarify his desires in his heart. More than positive thoughts, more than a couple coins, more than even his daily bread, Bartimaeus wanted to *see*. Jesus helped Bartimaeus raise the bar on what he wanted in life.

Maybe you feel like your big dream has gotten derailed so often it seems impossible. So instead of pursuing it and asking God to make it a reality, you lower your standard of what you hope to see and accomplish. Your desires become vague. Specificity leads to clarity; clarity leads to hope.

Vague vs. vulnerable

But hope can be scary. What if Jesus says no? I'm sure the thought entered Bartimaeus' mind. When he heard Jesus was approaching, he called out to Him, "Son of David!" Bartimaeus knew the reputation of Jesus. He knew the claims that Jesus was a descendant of King David, as the prophecies about the Messiah foretold. He had heard about Jesus healing the sick and blind. But he didn't want to get his hopes up. Vagueness can be a form of self-preservation. After all, if I don't make my heart's desire clear, then I won't be disappointed if it doesn't come true.

Jesus' call to specifics forced Bartimaeus to lay it all out on the line. "You called me the Son of David. You've heard what I can do. What do you want me to do *for you*?"

When you have a desire that by all other accounts seems unreasonable, but you approach the God who you believe can do the impossible, then, my friend, you're acting by faith.

Vague vs. faith-filled

"Alright, Mike, this was nice for Bartimaeus and all, but what about me nowadays? Jesus isn't just passing by and asking us all what He can do for us."

Well, you're right. We're not in the same position as Bartimaeus. We have an even *greater* invitation.

1 John 5:14-15 says, "And we are confident that he hears us whenever we ask for anything that pleases him. And since we know he hears us when we make our requests, we also know that he will give us what we ask for."

"Sweet! Okay then, so, God, provide a metallic black 2013 Aston Martin Vanquish with tan leather seats. Please and thank you."

That's . . . nice taste, but not what this verse means. This isn't a name-it-and-claim-it, blab-it-and-grab-it prayer verse. This is a promise that our faith, coming from an understanding of what is important to God, will never be fruitless. Faith doesn't mean being uncertain. In fact, it's the opposite. It means we can be confident God is a good, attentive, and generous God who says *yes* to whatever pleases Him.

If you're asking for winning lottery numbers, you'll probably be disappointed. But I hope you don't consider it a mere consolation prize to hear what pleases God is anything that makes you more like Jesus and brings Him glory. That is literally what we're here on earth to do.

And to that end, God has given us a blank check.

Whatever interruptions pop up, whatever turn of events force us to change course, whatever bad news derails our plan, the offer from your heavenly Father always stands.

"I am here. I love you. I can redeem this. Let's use this to grow closer together. So . . . what do you want me to do for you?"

CHAPTER 9

ALL THERE

Be a Pace-Setter

The reason interruptions can be so disorienting is they forcibly change our pace. When we don't control our pace, we hamstring our ability to listen. Listening is impossible when our pace is frantic.

Remember in Jesus' ministry of interruptions, time seemed to stop as He zoomed in and gave his full attention to a sick woman who reached out to Him in a crowd. Jesus was a pace-setter. In the hustle and bustle of people vying for his attention and creating interruptions left and right, He somehow managed to keep His sanity while helping people feel like they had His full attention.

This isn't supernatural. This is intentionally staying in the present.

Even in improv, staying in the present has two meanings. First, you the improvisor should stay in the moment—listening, thinking, taking the next best step now—and, second, keep the scene about what's happening in the present.

Be present.

While I was writing up an outline for this chapter, I was interrupted. My wife called on her way home from work to ask if we could spend her lunch break together. Not a bad interruption, of course, but still an interruption. But let me take an honest inventory of the thoughts which flew through my head when the phone rang:

"Aw, come on, I was just getting on a roll here. I wonder who it is? Probably the telemarketer from Omaha again. I wish I could finish this part I'm working on. Oh, it's Kelsey. Oh, no, I hope she's okay. Her low tire pressure light was on."

Then I answered the phone. She was fine. We decided we would eat leftover taco soup for lunch. But while I was still on the phone with her, I got another incoming call from someone from church. Commence inner thought sequence:

"Really? Right in the middle of my phone call? Should I take it now? No, I can wait until I'm done talking with Kelsey. But she and I might talk her entire way home. If I take the call now, I only have fifteen minutes anyway. Is that enough time? Last time this person and I talked it was like a half hour. Oh, right. I'm still on the phone with Kelsey. Say something, Mike!"

Again, this was a very mild set of interruptions in my day. But see how many thoughts went through my mind in a couple of seconds? When the interruptions are bigger, and the course derailed is even more significant, all these thoughts spin into a frenzied fog that makes it feel impossible to get your feet on the ground.

How do you clear the fog, set the pace in your mind, and dwell in the moment?

I'll address that question by asking another one: What did all my on-the-phone thoughts have in common? It's kind of a trick question. I'll let you off the hook and give you the answer. *They were all about me.* Yes, even the thoughts of concern for my wife were ultimately about me because they fed into my anxiety and didn't add value to her. And my thoughts about the incoming caller? Still about me—planning and thinking at the expense of being present in the current conversation.

So, what, Mike? Am I supposed to think about nothing? That sounds like some weird new age stuff.

No, no. I'm simply proposing a shift. Call it a mantra if you want, but it's called *Me to You.*

From me to you

I coached a group of pastors on connecting with their audience. A major component of connection is being present, so I opened the session with an exercise called *Me to You.* In this game, participants pass focus one at a time by gesturing to themselves, saying "me," and then making eye contact with another individual, pointing to them, and saying "to you." After a few turns go by, we take out the words. A few more turns go by and we cut out the pointing so the only way to shift focus is through eye contact.

As you can imagine, it takes a bit of concentration, as does being present. It's easy to feel a bit lost and confused in the later stages of the game, but that's when it's all the more important to control the pace by acknowledging your turn, making an intentional connection, and shifting the focus *from me to you.*

If your focus is on yourself, how an interruption affects you, and all the things you need to do to get back on track, you will feel outpaced. On the inside, you'll feel overwhelmed. On the outside, you'll look distracted. Next time you feel this way even a little bit, say to yourself, "From me. To you." Then, engage the active listening skills we talked about earlier. That's the goal of this shift: to put yourself into a position to listen to God and others.

Understand this is not about stuffing and ignoring your thoughts and problems. You would become so outwardly focused you would implode. Saying "from me" is an acknowledgment you have a reality that needs to be addressed. But then saying "to you" shifts your focus intentionally from how the interruption affects you, to the individual who needs your attention presently. From me. To you.

321 Improv had the honor of touring with Christian recording artist, Micah Tyler. Night after night, I would watch Micah meet and greet

hundreds of people after the show. What struck me was how intentionally *present* he was with each individual. I've seen too many public figures treat these situations like an assembly line. Shaking hands without eye contact. Saying, "Hey how are you" without smiling. But when fans interacted with Micah, even if it was for only a few seconds, they felt like they had his undivided attention. Because, well, they did.

After the tour, I asked him, "What helps you stay so present in those meet and greets?"

He shared his philosophy, "We only have what's in front of us to be faithful to. When I'm home, I want to be intentional in front of my family, try to be mindful of what's going on in their lives. When I show up to a concert, the people who show up may not have people in their home thinking about them the same way. They may not have people who are loving them, thinking about them, and trying to be mindful of them. If I leave my house, I want to be able to stand in front of those people and care for them as the people that God put in front of me on that day and be faithful to them."

When it comes to being present, we only have what's in front of us to be faithful to. It's not that what is elsewhere isn't important. But your opportunity is present. Right in front of you. And you might be the only present person they encounter all day.

Keep the scene in the present.

An improviser does well to stay in the moment with his scene partners—listening, connecting, responding—but if the scene is merely them reminiscing about something in the past or planning for something in the future, the scene won't go anywhere.

The other meaning of *stay in the present*, then, is *keep the scene in the present*. I have witnessed improv scenes where the entire time was spent planning something, like a mission.

"Okay, so I'll lift you up over the wall."

"Great. And then when I'm on the other side, I'll unlock the gate."

"What if there are guard dogs?"

"I brought a bratwurst just in case."

And so on, as you slowly realize the audience isn't actually watching those things happen. It's future talk. *Past* talk is equally pointless.

"Hey thanks for inviting me to your party last night."

"Oh, yeah, totally. Sorry you had to leave early."

"Yeah! I heard I missed out on the funniest thing of the night!"

"I know! Chad bet he could get from the kitchen to the garage without touching the floor. But he couldn't get across the living room, so he paid Tyler $20 to lay on the floor so he could walk on him!"

And so on, as you slowly realize the audience would rather watch that happen, rather than listen to people talk about it.

Nobody wants to watch a scene about you talking about what you did, or about what you are going to do. Just do it!

On a personal level, we tend to get stuck in scenes about the past or future. Depending on how you consider those times, you may relate to one or more of these mindsets:

- **Clinging** to the "better" past
- **Regretting** the past
- **Fantasizing** about a "better" future
- **Worrying** about the future

Clinging

You probably know somebody who revels in their *glory days*. Being a starter on the high school football team. Traveling the globe before getting married and having kids. And there's certainly nothing wrong about enjoying wonderful memories. But it's easy for us to put these memories on a pedestal and compare our present circumstances to them. And then, we are mere steps away from discontentment. When we glorify our glory days, we resent our present days.

Don't have too narrow a view of what your glory days may be. Sure, they might be decades ago, starring a younger, more energetic, fuller-head-of-hair you, or they might be yesterday. Before you got sick. Before the notice appeared on your desk. Before the phone

When we glorify our glory days, we resent our present days.

call. And your mind becomes fixed on the way things used to be.

The funny thing (well, the sad thing) about clinging to the past is there's nothing truly there to cling to. And while you're grasping at nothing, you're missing out on what is present.

You want to know what made your glory days so fulfilling and memorable? At the time, you were present in them. Be present today. Make today a glory day.

Regretting

When Jeremy first joined 321 Improv, his major struggle always came after the show. At dinner or on his way home, he would inevitably think of something he wished he had said or done in the show to make it even funnier. We joked about it; we even called these sessions "Jeremy's Regret Corner." But for a while, the regret really ate at him. I can relate; I went through the same thing. So have most improvisers, I'm guessing.

We give *would've*, *could've*, and *should've* so much airtime in our minds they hinder our ability to do anything in the present. Now, I'm all about learning from past mistakes. And we should consider them for the sake of personal growth. But regret sinks in when our thoughts about the past overstep those bounds and start to have a voice. *That was so stupid of me. I'm better than that! If I hadn't done that, everything would be fine now.*

With thoughts like those floating around, it will be difficult to make the choices or take the chances you need to in the present. When you give regret a voice, you give the past power over your present.

Fantasizing

The future can be equally distracting. Thoughts of a brighter future can become a go-to retreat from the present.

Mike, you can't possibly be saying that hope is a bad thing.

Oh, absolutely not. I'm not even talking about hope. I'm talking about daydreaming to the point of day-wasting. I'm talking about keeping your mind so far into the future you're not taking any steps now to get there.

—⁓—

In my early twenties, I was looking for a refreshing outdoor hobby. One spring vacation on a Florida beach, as I watched kites dive and swoop, inspiration struck. I was going to be a kite guy!

I bought a parafoil kite (fellow kite-people, you understand what I'm talking about). Its maiden flight started off as nothing short of a spiritual experience. I harnessed the strength of the wind with my fingertips! I fixed my eyes upward and imagined myself at that altitude, looking down at the awestruck beachgoers. Looking back down at myself at the other end of the string. What if I went higher? I let the string out further and further until there was no more wrapped around the handle.

Apparently, the direction and strength of the wind was different up where the kite was, compared to where I stood. The kite took some sudden dives and turns. The string, which now extended over a significant stretch of the beach, was at a lower angle, and I couldn't guarantee it wouldn't clothesline some nearby volleyball players.

The kite continued its unpredictable acrobatics. I frantically tried to reel it in against the strong gusts while running away from the shore in an attempt to not cause bodily harm to anyone. Bodily harm, however, is exactly what you get when you run barefoot, without looking, on the rough, rocky, shelly portion of the beach near the tree line. As I kept my eyes upward at the kite, my foot caught a twisted root, and down I went.

We tend to view hope like a kite. We fix our gaze up, up, and away. We imagine what it would be like to be up there. But, to our detriment, we often ignore the very ground beneath our feet. Kite-like hope can lift our spirits for a brief time, but it's no way to live.

Fortunately, as believers in Christ, we can have hope like an anchor. Check out Hebrews 6:18-19. "We who have fled to him for refuge can have great confidence as we hold to the hope that lies before us. This hope is a strong and trustworthy anchor for our souls."

When you set anchor, you don't gaze downward longingly at it. Instead, you are assured no matter what happens at the surface, you are secure. You can go about your work with confidence. In verse 11 of the same chapter, the author expresses what present actions we can take with our anchor-like hope: "Our great desire is that you will keep on loving others as long as life lasts, in order to make certain that what you hope for will come true."

When we get derailed by unexpected life events, it's natural to yearn idly for a better future and call it hope. But sincere hope in the Lord is an anchor that keeps us grounded and motivated to know the work we do will not be in vain.

Worrying

For some, though, hope may not be in the forecast. You may spend your mental energy thinking about the future, and not in the inspirational way. You worry.

Jesus has some words on worry, and I'd like to get right to them without any interruption from me:

> That is why I tell you not to worry about everyday life—whether you have enough food and drink, or enough clothes to wear. Isn't life more than food, and your body more than clothing? Look at the birds. They don't plant or harvest or store food in barns, for your heavenly Father feeds them. And aren't you far more valuable to him than they are?

Can all your worries add a single moment to your life?

And why worry about your clothing? Look at the lilies of the field and how they grow. They don't work or make their clothing, yet Solomon in all his glory was not dressed as beautifully as they are. And if God cares so wonderfully for wildflowers that are here today and thrown into the fire tomorrow, he will certainly care for you. Why do you have so little faith?

So, don't worry about these things, saying, 'What will we eat? What will we drink? What will we wear?' These things dominate the thoughts of unbelievers, but your heavenly Father already knows all your needs. Seek the Kingdom of God above all else, and live righteously, and he will give you everything you need.

So, don't worry about tomorrow, for tomorrow will bring its own worries. Today's trouble is enough for today. (Matthew 6:25-34)

Three times in this passage alone, Jesus says not to worry. For so many of us, worry has been a pet sin. Some people consider worry as a responsible thing to do, like a mantle they must wear for the ones they love. Some see their worry as a barometer of how aware they are of the circumstances. But no matter how you cut it, Jesus tells us worry is a result of having little faith, and makes us no different than unbelievers.

It shouldn't be a surprise Jesus' antidote for worry involves present action. Seek the Kingdom of God and live righteously.

Shift your focus from the future to what you have control over in the present. Specifically, pour value into God's work in the lives of those around you (that's what it means to seek the Kingdom of God), and grow in your character and relationship with Jesus to become more like Him with every twist and turn of life. If you do this, God promises to give you everything you need. Now *that's* a promise you can sink your anchor into!

The God of the Present.

Jesus' ministry on earth was surprisingly brief— only about three years long. But in that time, He was overwhelmingly present with the people in front of Him. And for you numbers-people, I brought stats. Check this out.

I went through the book of Mark and looked at each time Jesus spoke. I counted each sentence (or group of sentences, if they shared the same thought) and noted if it was in the past, present, or future tense. Of Jesus' *thought units* in the book of Mark, 12% are past tense (half of which are parables taught as past-tense stories), 28% are future tense (a third of which are in one long message prophesying the end times), and 60% are in the present tense.

When you look at Jesus' interactions with people, the vast majority of them are about in-the-moment invitations, responses, and instructions. Even when Jesus talked about the past, it was usually to tell a story with a present application. And if He talked about the future, it was to equip His listeners to be able to take appropriate action now.

Jesus went about His ministry with urgency but set the pace with a focus on the present, giving His all to the ones in front of Him. It's no surprise the Son of God was so present, considering the name God gave Himself.

Thousands of years earlier, Moses was in the hot seat, and it wasn't because of the burning bush in front of him. It was because God was telling him to return to Egypt and rally God's people, the local slaves, and march out of slavery into a land they could call theirs. But . . . Moses was banished from Egypt for murder, and the Israelite slaves only knew Moses as spoiled Egyptian royalty, if they remembered him at all after his forty years of herding sheep in exile.

Understandably, Moses was drawing heavily on past *if-onlys* and future *what-ifs* to try to convince God he shouldn't be the one to go to Egypt. We pick up the conversation in Exodus 3:13-14.

> But Moses protested, "If I go to the people of Israel and tell them, 'The God of your ancestors has sent me to you,' they will ask me, 'What is his name?' Then what should I tell them?" God replied to Moses, "I am who I am. Say this to the people of Israel: I AM has sent me to you."

I love the verse that follows. "This is my eternal name, my name to remember for all generations." Does that blow your mind a little bit? God's name for himself is I AM, the most present name possible, and it is His name *forever*! Wherever you are, I AM!

Do you believe in I AM? Or do you believe in I WAS?

I WAS with you before your accident. I WAS your loving Father before your parents' divorce. I WAS your God while you were a kid going to church.

Maybe your god is I WILL. I WILL bless you once you clean up your life. I WILL show up in your life when you show up to church. I WILL love you when you become lovable.

Allow me to introduce you to I AM, who is our refuge and strength, and an *ever-present* help in trouble (Psalm 46:1).

Who has loved you since before time itself? I AM.

Who will never leave you or forsake you? I AM.

Who put aside heaven, taking the name Immanuel, or *God With Us*, to become like us so our broken relationship with our Creator could be healed? I AM.

Since we are created in the image of God, or I AM, could it be we are most like Him when we are present with those whom He has placed in front of us?

CHAPTER 10

THE TRUTH GAME

Be a Truth-Teller

"Package delivery for Paula?"

"I'm sorry, I think you have the wrong house." Pause.

Okay, improviser. You started the scene as a delivery person. Not bad. But now "Paula" here, trying to inject some conflict into the scene, has made it difficult to continue. What do you do?

You can't argue with her. "Nope, I'm sure I have the right address." A back-and-forth argument doesn't go anywhere. Instead, you'll have to accept that okay, I guess you have the wrong house. Remember *yes, and?* But then what?

In improv, it can be disorienting when somebody says or does something seemingly irrational. In such cases, it's tempting to pull yourself out of the situation by making a joke or doing something equally irrational.

But have you ever laughed and said, "It's funny because it's true?"

Why is that? Considered by many to be the "bible" of improv, *Truth in Comedy* by Del Close and Charna Halpern, says, "The truth is funny. Honest discovery, observation, and reaction is better than contrived invention."[1]

So, in these moments when you don't know what to do, look for what's true. It's time to play a game called The Truth Game. It's simple, but it's not necessarily easy. Ask yourself, *If this is true, what else is true?*

Unpause.

Well, if it's true I have the wrong house, maybe it's because I'm still new at this.

"Sorry, it's my first week on the job."

"Yeah, that's the third time this week!"

Well, if that's true, that means I've been here before and am familiar with this house. And if that's true, then maybe there's a reason I keep coming back.

"While I'm here . . . do you have any more of those muffins you baked yesterday?"

"Um . . . yes? I think I have a couple left" (Fortunately, Paula is starting to *yes, and* a little better now).

If that's true, then what else is true? I want a muffin. I want to stay and visit. I got this job so I can go around, meet people, and make friends and eat their baked goods.

"Great! I've got some time. Let's sit on the porch and chat over some muffins. In fact, I think in this package here . . . yep! It's a tea set!"

And voila, you were able to discover a usable (albeit quirky) character and motivation amid an unexpected roadblock.

Part of the joy of improv is whatever you say, that's what becomes true. If only that was the case in real life. The reality is we live in a world where truth goes on with or without us. When life takes an unexpected turn, it's easy to forget what's true. Some things are *still* true from before the interruption. Some things are *now* true because of the interruption. The more we can identify truths in those two categories, the clearer we can see the appropriate action to take. When you feel thrown off, ask yourself, *If this is true, what else is true?*

If this is true, what else is true?

Just before sending this book to print, the world was in the throes of the once-in-a-lifetime pandemic known as COVID-19. Prior to this, I shared another personal example in this section. But the outbreak offered a narrative the entire world could relate to. As a communicator, you don't often get to share an example with worldwide relevance, so I'm taking advantage because I can.

Many were affected personally and deeply by the coronavirus itself. Many more were affected by the economic impacts of the quarantine. All were affected in some way. Personally, due to my work being in the entertainment industry, my income was cut to zero. School was cancelled, so I was thrust into immediate employment as homeschool teacher. Amidst the waves of fear, worry, and uncertainty, my wife and I had to play a game. The Truth Game. What was *now* true? What was *still* true?

It was *now* true the entire world was experiencing this, so financial grace was being given for all sorts of difficult payments. It was now true I had more time to devote to important things: my family, my church, even this book. It was *still* true we had technology to connect with friends through the quarantine. It was still true we had our health and our home. And even if the world changed so those things were no longer true, we knew that God is good and He would provide.

The Truth Game has become a go-to in my family when things don't go according to plan. Why does it work? Because there are some truths about truth that make it, well, truth. I'll call them *Truth Truths.* And they all come from what I have found to be the ultimate source of truth.

Truth Truths

Truth guides us.

On the road with 321 Improv, one thing that always makes us chuckle is when, after a show, our sponsor asks if we know how to get to the restaurant for dinner.

"Applebee's? Yep, we'll see you there."

"You sure you know the way?"

"We've got it in the GPS. Looks close."

"Yeah, it's close. So, what you're going to want to do is turn right at the end of this road. At the intersection with the Sonic, turn left. You'll pass a Culver's and Buffalo Wild Wings, and then Applebee's will be on your right."

We have to smile and nod, as they mean well. But really, we navigated from our individual homes all the way to this church in Kearney, Nebraska. I think we can avoid getting lost on the way to the Applebee's around the corner!

But can you imagine navigating to the Applebee's in Kearny, Nebraska without a GPS?* Sure, there are paper maps you could use. And you could follow the directions given by people who know the way. But in each of these cases, you are relying on truth outside of yourself. What other choice do you have? You might have a general sense of which highways will bring you toward Nebraska. But if you've never been there, you're

---

* If you live in Kearny, Nebraska, feel free to ignore this part.

still relying on the maps you were taught. There is truth outside your experience. When traveling outside your experience, that truth is the only guide.

In a culture that celebrates embracing and following *your* truth, it's not surprising to see so many people feeling lost, confused, and reaching extremely different conclusions.

What's true is we weren't made solely for this world. Jesus Himself acknowledged this as He prayed—for *us*, can you believe it?—to His Father. "They do not belong to this world any more than I do. Make them holy by your truth; teach them your word, which is truth" (John 17:16-17).

> There is truth outside your experience. When traveling outside your experience, that truth is the only guide.

We are in unfamiliar territory and bound for an eternity we've never experienced before. You better believe we need a guide!

Fortunately, we have a God who guarantees His Word as truth. "Lead me by your truth and teach me," the psalmist David writes, "for you are the God who saves me" (Psalm 25:5). And that's a truth we can follow to our grave.

Truth grounds us.

Philippians 4:8 is a verse I read every day without even trying. My wife repurposed an antique window and painted its words on the panes. This window sits on a little table by my front door, so I see it whenever I leave the house. "And now, dear brothers and sisters, one final thing. Fix your thoughts on what is true, and honorable, and right, and pure, and lovely, and admirable. Think about things that are excellent and worthy of praise."

It's a strict but effective filter for what we let sit in our minds. But looking at the context of the chapter, Paul is prescribing how to find peace and freedom from worry. Immediately previous in Paul's letter, we find another often-quoted passage: "Don't worry about anything; instead, pray about everything. Tell God what you need and thank him for all he has done." (Philippians 4:6).

When I read this verse quickly, I get the general impression, *Okay, don't worry. Pray instead.* But we can't ignore the call to be thankful! Why? Because gratitude serves as a reminder about what is true in your life.

I had the privilege of spending nearly three decades knowing my great-grandmother, Eva. The impression she left on those who knew her was a legacy of gratitude. When she and her husband Will had to move from the house he had built decades earlier into an assisted living community, Eva was thankful for the many years they spent together in their home. When Will got sick and had to live in the nearby nursing home, Eva was thankful she could walk to visit him every day for lunch. When Will passed away, she was thankful for the seventy years of marriage they had shared. And through it all, she was thankful for the love of "my Jesus," as she was fond of saying.

I have never met a more unshakable person than my great-grandmother. She chose gratitude at every turn, so she never lost sight of the most important truth in her life: Jesus loved her. Gratitude kept her grounded, and it can keep you grounded, too.

Maybe that's why gratitude stands for Grounding Reminder About Truth In Trials, Under . . . D-Dinosaur . . . Extinction. . . . Man, I really thought I was on to something there . . . ruined the moment. Ah, well.

> Gratitude serves as a reminder about what is true in your life.

Failed acronym aside, next time you're struggling to remind yourself of what's true, try thinking of things you are thankful for. You might be taking for granted some blessings that remain true in your life, despite the circumstances.

Truth guards us.

"Stand your ground, putting on the belt of truth" (Ephesians 6:14). As Paul penned (quilled?) these words, he was in a Roman prison, under the watch of an armored guard. Without much else to look at, Paul was inspired to equate each piece of a soldier's armor with a different attribute of a Christian's defense against Satan's attacks.

In Paul's day, a soldier's belt served three critical functions: (1) it supported the scabbard, where the sword was kept, (2) it held strips of leather for added protection, and (3) it securely fastened the other pieces of armor.

Likewise, reminding ourselves of what's true (of our circumstances, as well as of God's promises) serves to support and cinch together all our defenses against the deceit and self-defeating thoughts that accompany life's disappointments.

"I can't make it through this." False. I can do everything through Christ who gives me strength. Philippians 4:13.

"God can't love me, after what I've done." False. When we were still sinners, Christ died for us. Romans 5:8.

"Nobody can help me." False. Come to me, and I will give you rest. Matthew 11:28.

Doubts? There's a truth for that.

Insecurity? There's a truth for that.

Study what God has promised to be true in His Word. Arm yourself with it every day. Write it on your bathroom mirror. Make it the background on your phone. Have it tattooed on your wrist if you must. Let the truth of God guard you, and boldly live in light of that truth.

Truth guides, grounds, and guards us. What a comfort when the unexpected things in life make us feel lost, off-balanced, and vulnerable! Our next best step begins by reminding ourselves what is true—not what we wish was true, not what used to be true—simply what is true right now. And then, with that in mind, what else is true? We need to let the truth inform our thoughts and our actions.

That seems trite, doesn't it? But what's the alternative? Our thoughts will come from somewhere. If not the truth, then what? The answer is a matter of life and death. And no, I'm not being dramatic. Check out Romans 8:6. "Letting your sinful nature control your mind leads to death. But letting the Spirit control your mind leads to life and peace." There are only two options here. Either you intentionally train your thoughts toward peace and life, or your thoughts drift toward anxiety and death.

Your mind is a battlefield, and as such, you need a battle plan. Tighten your belt. Here we go!

Truth Training Battle Plan

Step 1: Capture your thoughts.

Untruths, doubts, and criticisms plague your mind every day and dampen your ability to take your next best step. But you are not a helpless victim of your thoughts. Paul puts the power in your hands with some strong action words, which I'll emphasize here: "We *demolish* arguments and every pretension that sets itself up against the knowledge of God, and we *take captive* every thought to *make it obedient* to Christ" (2 Corinthians 10:5, NIV, emphasis mine).

This process isn't about holding hands, thinking positive thoughts, and emanating good vibes. It's aggressive; it's intentional; it's persistent, got-to-get-another-one, Hacksaw-Ridge-level intensity in the name of Jesus. Slap the hand of deceit as it reaches for your truth cookies. Slap it hard. To the best of your ability, force every thought through the filter of Philippians 4:8 we talked about. Is it true? Is it pure? Is it excellent? No? Kick it to the curb!

Step 2: Write new stories.

Harris III, Master Illusionist and long-time friend of 321 Improv, challenges his audiences to recapture their childlike wonder and sense of imagination. He doesn't believe imagination is lost in adulthood; it simply changes forms. "Worry is a misuse of imagination," he shares. Somewhere along our path to adulthood, we've twisted our imagination from a creativity-machine into a worry-factory.

In light of an uncertain future, you have a choice. Worry is a response; it is not an emotion. You may say, "I feel worried." But really, you're *choosing* to worry. You may have made the choice to worry so quickly and so often it *feels* like an emotion, but it is not. Worrying is telling yourself stories about what hasn't happened yet and living as if they are true.

I don't know about you, but I have felt more pain, lost more sleep, and clenched more teeth because of these stories than because of any reality. I'd be embarrassed to know how many times my wife or daughter has died in my mind because of an unanswered phone call. I have, no joke, written eulogies in my mind for funerals of people who are still alive. It's a problem!

If you struggle with worry, it's time to tell yourself new stories. Use your imagination to create the best-case scenario instead of the worst. Visualize the good that could happen instead of the bad. Why isn't she answering the phone? She must be having a fun time with her friends. Write stories of life instead of death and read them avidly.

Step 3: Let God change you.

Steps 1 and 2 require active effort on your part, but that doesn't mean you have to go about this mind transformation alone. Look at Romans 12:2. "Don't copy the behavior and customs of this world, but let God transform you into a new person by changing"—what?—The way you act? The way you appear? No! By changing "the way you think." Then what? "Then you will learn to know God's will for you, which is good and pleasing and perfect."

Notice the word "let." *Let* God transform you. He's not going to force change on you. He stands at the door and knocks (Revelation 3:20). He's not kicking it down. Have you ever invited God to change the way you think? Maybe you've been a Christian for a long time, but your thought life is characterized by the same kinds of worry, judgment, and self-defeat that plague the rest of the world. And you wonder where God is through it all? Have you bothered to invite Him in?

God loves you. His will for you is good, pleasing, and perfect. If this is true, what else is true?

*** COMMERCIAL BREAK ***

We once again interrupt your program to bring you another exciting offer!

Do you like surprises? Who doesn't! Surprise parties, surprise gifts, surprise arguments with friends and coworkers when you thought you were on the same page? Well, if you can't get enough surprises in your life and are craving the most time-consuming, relationship-breaking, day-derailing surprises, boy, do I have a product for you!

Hi, I'm Chef Mike, with a revolutionary new tool that will help you create surprises at work, in the car, or in the comfort of your home. Introducing, the Shock Crock 2000!

For the most delicious surprises, start by adding a generous amount of assumptions. Other inferior products will tell you to consider *alternatives*, to prepare yourself in case your assumptions are incorrect. But not with the Shock Crock 2000! With our patented Alternatives Filter, you don't have to worry about if your assumptions are incorrect. Set it and forget it!

The Shock Crock 2000's AirLock Lid ensures no pesky truths and input from other people will leak in and disturb the process. In a short amount of time, your assumptions will turn into expectations. Now, at this point, you may be tempted to communicate your expectations and share them with others. Trust me—and this is incredibly important—DO NOT communicate your expectations with other people! This will flatten your surprise faster than a souffle with the oven door open.

When your expectations have had enough time to solidify in private, sit back and wait. Soon enough, you will get to experience your very own surprise! Check out these reviews from some of our millions of satisfied customers:

> "I wanted my husband to start dinner before I got home, but I didn't ask! I just assumed he would be thoughtful of me after my long day. Boy was I shocked! Thanks, Shock Crock 2000!"
>
> —Kristen A., Dubuque, IA

> "With the Shock Crock 2000, I surprised myself with how quickly I lashed out at my coworker for how loud he talks on the phone! I assumed he knew, I expected him to know how it bothers me, and two weeks later, I was yelling at him! Highly recommended!"
>
> —Adam P., Sheboygan, WI

> "The Shock Crock 2000 takes out the guesswork of "if" I'm going to be surprised, while keeping the thrill of guessing "when!" I bought one for all my best friends!"
>
> —Rachel W., Kalamazoo, MI

Why *talk* when you can Shock Crock? Order now!

*** BACK TO THE PROGRAM ***

CHAPTER 11
DO SOMETHING!

Be an Action-Taker

Boy, Mike, if I were up there on stage, I wouldn't know what to do! I'd be worried I'd do the wrong thing!

You want to know a little secret? Yeah? Lean in. Close. Ready?

There is no such thing as wrong.

What? Mabel! Grab me my book-burning torch! We've got heresy to purge! I can't believe I had to endure ten whole chapters before getting to this! Who does this Mike guy think he is?

Whoa, whoa, easy there. Put down the lighter fluid. Let me explain. I don't mean *wrong* in the moral sense. I'm talking about this idea of *the wrong choice* that cripples so many people from choosing anything at all for fear of choosing incorrectly.

In that sense, it should be freeing to realize there is no such thing as wrong.

Okay, fine. I see how that could be the case in improv. But not in real life. In real life, there are definitely right choices and wrong choices, right? Right?

Honestly, I'm not so sure there are. At least not as drastic as we make them out to be. What's more likely is you find yourself paralyzed by an *illusion* of a right choice, or even a "best" choice, and you end up not taking any action at all.

So, the advice given in improv class can be given to you: do something!

It's hard. I totally get it. It's easier said than done. Especially at certain times in our life, the necessary first step feels like it has a cinder block tied to it. I've identified some common choke points where *do something* is a tough pill to swallow. Fortunately, there is encouragement to be found in each situation.

Chokepoint 1: The Valley

Ezra was a prophet who came onto the scene in one of the lowest points in the history of God's people, the Israelites. They had been released from exile, and they returned home to find the temple to God destroyed. The laws God had put in place to protect them had been ignored and forgotten. Most notably, the Israelites had married into pagan families and adopted their harmful religious practices.

Ezra taught and pleaded with God's people to the point he was weeping bitterly in front of the temple. He drew quite the crowd, who began weeping themselves. The people were repentant, but the cry-fest continued until one man, Shecaniah, approached Ezra.

"We have been unfaithful to our God, for we have married these pagan women of the land. But in spite of this, there is hope for Israel. Get up, for it is your duty to tell us how to proceed in setting things straight. We are behind you, so be strong and take action" (Ezra 10:2, 4).

Ezra was swamped with regret on behalf of the people and burdened by the responsibility to lead them. When we're in our low points, our valleys, it can be difficult to see the way out and know what to do next. Do you have a Shecaniah in your life who can come alongside you and provide perspective? I hope so. If not, in the meantime, allow me to borrow a page from Shecaniah's book.

Acknowledge the valley.

Shecaniah started by acknowledging that, yes, things were bad. In the case of the Israelites, their sin caused a major rift between them and God. Your valley might not be a consequence of sin. If it is, by all means, put this book down right now and ask for God's forgiveness. But maybe it's a valley season. Whatever the case, acknowledging your circumstance is the first step of climbing out of it.

Remind yourself of the truth of hope.

"In spite of this," Shecaniah encouraged, "there is hope." Hope lies in the truth of God's promises. For Ezra, hope could have been found in the promise of 2 Chronicles 7:14. "Then if my people who are called by my name will humble themselves and pray and seek my face and turn from their wicked ways, I will hear from heaven and will forgive their sins and restore their land." For you, God promises comfort in trials (2 Corinthians 1:3-4), peace (Philippians 4:6-7), provision (Matthew 6:33), and many more. Study His Word and draw on the hope He is offering.

Get up.

The first two steps were mental. We start, as Peter compels us, by preparing our minds for action (1 Peter 1:13). The next two steps, though, is where it gets physical. Ezra needed a change of posture. He had been in full mourning mode, face-down on the steps of the temple. But considering the reminder of hope, he couldn't stay there. He had to get up. Hope ignites action. Before you can walk, let alone run, you first need to get up.

Hope ignites action.

Be strong and act.

Shecaniah promised Ezra that he and his friends were behind him and would support his action. This encouragement reminds me of when Joshua took over for Moses to lead God's people into their new land. A major leadership change at the doorstep of the enemy? Joshua needed strength to act, so God Himself approached him. The call to be strong wasn't only friendly encouragement. "This is my command—be strong and courageous! Do not be afraid or discouraged. For the Lord your God is with you wherever you go" (Joshua 1:9). When God calls you to action, it's a command! Be strong and courageous. Take action. The Lord is behind you. And step by step, you'll find your way out of the valley.

Chokepoint 2: The Mountain

But a valley isn't the only terrain that threatens to nail your feet to the floor. Surprisingly, the high of a mountaintop experience can make it equally difficult to take your next best step.

There was a literal mountain special to God's people after He freed them from slavery in Egypt. You see, from the moment they left Egypt, they had been constantly on the move. God used a fiery cloud to signal when they would set up camp and when they would pack it up again. When it moved, they moved. When it stopped, they stopped[1]. It went on like this for two months! You can imagine their relief when the cloud settled over Mount Sinai and didn't move for *a whole year!* This year was marked by consistency, predictability, provision, protection, teaching, and a front row seat to God's display of his glory. In fact, Moses had so much "face time" with God on that mountain, his face literally glowed![2]

Have you enjoyed a mountaintop experience? A season where everything seems to go right? Projects go according to plan; prayers get answered the way you hope; finances are steady and sufficient. Good news comes through phone calls and emails without any flip side to ruin the enjoyment. God seems closer somehow. You might be able to relate to Moses' glow that warms your heart and brightens your outlook. Don't you wish you could stay there forever?

The Israelites probably did. Was it refreshing? Sure. Was it recharging? Absolutely. But was it the promised land? No, it was not. Likewise, your mountaintop isn't your home. It's bittersweet to hear what God told His people— "You have stayed at this mountain long enough. It is time to break camp and move on" (Deuteronomy 1:6-7).

That can be hard to swallow, can't it? After all, where do you go after leaving a mountain? Another valley, eventually. And that's not fun to look forward to. But that's why it's all the more important to refresh yourself at the mountain and be ready to move when God calls you to move. Because, like it or not, God is moving with or without you.

—⁂—

My family was gifted an opportunity to go whale watching off the coast of Boston. I'll be honest, we weren't optimistic. We had been once before, and on that trip, we saw a dolphin. A dolphin. The "See a whale or your money back!" guarantee wasn't helpful either; apparently dolphins are a type of whale. Marine biologists: one. Domeny family: zero.

Our second experience started off similarly disappointing. We were on the port side* of the boat when we heard the tour guide over the intercom. "On the starboard side,** I think we have a rare Finback whale! Yes, it is! That's the second largest whale in the world! *Wow!* What a close encounter! That was amazing!"

You could feel the boat tilt to the right as everybody scrambled to the starboard rail. When we finally managed to catch a peek at the water, all we could see was some swirling foam. We stayed there, determined not to miss anything again.

Not long after, we heard, "Port side! Humpback whale! And its tail fin is in the air! Wow!" Commence round two of shuffling across the boat only to spy a seagull.

Eventually, we did figure out the rhythm of the whales and the way the captain maneuvered the boat to position us the best he could. We were rewarded with a number of successful sightings. But I had to chuckle at myself and the way I had fixated on the place the whale was last seen. The whale, the boat, the waves—everything was moving! Yet there I stayed, watching only where the whale *was*, and expecting to see an encore.

---

* That's the left side, for you landlubbers.
** Yes, that's sailor-speak for, *Mike and his family are missing out.*

When God acts in a powerful, memorable way, it's tempting to want to live on the mountain and wait for him with eager expectation to do it again. But, as TD Jakes warns, "God is a moving God. If you don't move with him, you end up worshipping where God was."[3]

Don't Do Nothing!

God's call to action is an ever-present one. We don't have the option of doing nothing. James warns us "it is sin to know what you ought to do and then not do it" (James 4:17).

In fact, James is real keen on the idea of our actions reflecting our faith and obedience. It's easy to read a Bible passage with a trendy background on social media, or listen to a sound bite from a sermon, and nod and share it without it affecting your life. But as James insists:

"Don't just listen to God's word. You must do what it says. Otherwise, you are only fooling yourselves. For if you listen to the word and don't obey, it is like glancing at your face in a mirror. You see yourself, walk away, and forget what you look like. But if you look carefully into the perfect law that sets you free, and if you do what it says and don't forget what you heard, then God will bless you for doing it." (James 1:22-25)

He goes on to escalate the point even further. "So, you see, faith by itself isn't enough. Unless it produces good deeds, it is dead and useless. Just as the body is dead without breath, so also faith is dead without good works" (James 2:17, 26).

Don't misunderstand James here. He's *not* saying faith by itself isn't enough *for salvation*. We know salvation is by faith alone; He's way past that. James, rather, is lighting a match under the professing Christian who is still sitting on his hands, waiting for the world to change.

If you feel like your faith hasn't done you any good, maybe the problem is *you* haven't done any good.

Fortunately, when God calls us to action, He never intends for us to have it all figured out or to know exactly where we're going. He invites us improvisers into the scene with Him. So, we, as the old improv adage goes, bring a brick, not a cathedral.

Bring a brick.

I don't know who in the improv world coined this rule, but it continues to be one of my favorite sayings on stage and in life.

Remember in Chapter 2, I introduced this idea in the context of keeping a loose grip on your plans. The emphasis was to avoid coming into a relationship with a cathedral—grand, elaborate plans with no room for others' input.

Now, as we talk about taking action, I'd like to highlight the first part of that saying— "bring a brick." Sometimes, you feel so far from envisioning a cathedral you can't even imagine taking a first action step. For you, I can shift the emphasis and say, "Just bring a *brick*; don't worry about the cathedral."

What is your brick? Where your willingness and your value meet, there you will find your brick. When you are willing to act, and you recognize the value you can add, you'll find yourself with a brick in hand. Willingness to serve and value to offer. Bringing your brick is your first responsibility, and something (maybe the only thing) you have absolute control over.

- Bring a brick to the meeting, even if you don't have a solution.
- Bring a brick to your friend, even if it's been a while.
- Bring a brick to your marriage, even if you don't think your spouse will bring theirs.

Bring a brick, not a cathedral. And when you do, guess what? There *still* won't be a cathedral. Bring a brick again tomorrow. And the next day. And every day for a year. And even then, you might look at your work and only see a wall. Instead of being discouraged by the lack of cathedral, celebrate the wall! Celebrate the bricks others are contributing. And when you've celebrated, bring another brick. Brick in hand, keep taking what you see to be the next best step.

But how?

Okay, I'm convinced taking action is better than staying where I am. And I've got my brick, I guess. But I'm still not sure what to do.

I totally understand. And really, your exact action step is between you and God. Maybe your best next step is to talk with Him and have a conversation with your caring Creator. But I will say this is true no matter what you end up doing. *How is more important than what.*

Wear the vest.

Colossians 3:17 leaves our *what* pretty wide open. "And whatever you do or say, do it as a representative of the Lord Jesus, giving thanks through him to God the Father." What do you do or say? Paul here doesn't care. Whatever it is, though, make sure you represent Jesus.

By nature, I'm not a confrontational person. My brother works in the security industry, and the stories he tells about having to confront people both inspire and terrify me. So, at a Helicopter Easter Egg Drop event at my church, you can imagine my hesitation to agree to work crowd control. A mass of parents and their kids pressed up against the gate, trying to get a head start. Older kids wanted to run with the younger kids so they could get their eggs earlier.

Parents wanted to use baskets they brought instead of the standard-sized bags we provided.

It was a people-pleaser's nightmare. If I said yes to everyone who asked, it would compromise the safety and orderliness of the event. But I had a secret weapon—a yellow vest.

My vest not only showed other people I represented my church, but—more importantly—my vest reminded me of the authority I had as a representative. And you better believe as I stood at the front of the crowd, or as I walked around the event, I tried to display every bit of the loving, relevant, and life-giving reputation my church strives for. But I also felt empowered to say or do what was necessary for the good of who I was representing, even if it was out of my personal comfort zone.

When you became a Christ follower, you were given a vest. It's both a responsibility and a privilege. It's a responsibility in the fact that everything you do or say should line up with the reputation of Christ. But it's also a privilege, as you have the freedom and the authority to speak and act freely on His behalf.

Do and say whatever you want, but remember you're wearing His vest!

Keep your eyes up.

My daughter was a late walker. She simply wasn't interested. I've since learned it's her personality to watch and study and only try something when she feels good and ready. When she finally decided for the first time to stand up and walk, she put her hands behind her back like a supervisor patrolling the floor. "This isn't all that hard! I can literally do it with my hands behind my back!" But what she *couldn't* do with her hands behind her back was to protect her face when she fell forward.

Caring father that I am, whenever she got up to walk, I pushed aside each little toy and blanket that could trip her up. She kept her eyes on me, and I made the path clear for her.

"In all your ways acknowledge him, and he will make straight your paths" (Proverbs 3:6, ESV).

We have a Father who promises to do the same for us. In *all* your ways—again, God isn't expecting you to guess the correct thing to say or do. *Whatever* you do—acknowledge Him. Keep your eyes on Him. Defer to His will. Lean on Him for wisdom. Give Him the glory for each success. And He will make your paths straight.

We tend to think of life like a maze with one correct path and a whole bunch of wrong ones—twists, turns, and obstacles along the way. This mindset is what makes it so frustrating when something comes up unexpectedly to throw us off course. But what if you lift your focus off the maze and onto your Maker? Soon, you'll find that regardless of whether you decide to turn right or left, God straightens your path so it leads closer to Him.

———〰———

Like I said, *do something* is easier said than done. So is everything worth doing. But so much fulfillment and healing comes from stepping out in faith and walking with Jesus through this unscripted life, your enemy's best bet is to try to keep you from doing anything in the first place. He'll use whatever tactic suits you best—worry, pride, insecurity. He might even say exactly *what* you do *really* matters, and you should make sure you get everything exactly right before you do anything.

Or you can—and trust me on this—pray, trust God, and do something.

CHAPTER 12
ALL IN!

Be an All-Giver

Well, here we are at the last chapter of this book. Can you allow me to get personal for a minute before we wrap this up?

Thank you for sticking with me this far. It has been an absolute privilege to be able to share these thoughts. It's been an exciting journey to see how God has tied together truths from my two passions of improv and the Bible, and I'm humbled you have walked with me through its entirety.

It's this idea of entirety, of 100%, and of going all-in I'd like to end on. So, don't put the book down now! That would be ironic and sad.

—ɯ—

I'm certainly not the best improviser to ever grace a stage. I'm not the quickest thinker; I'll stumble over my words. But if there's one thing I do well as an improviser, it's going all-in.

I love the rush of being fully immersed in what I'm portraying on stage. Physically, vocally, mentally—I jump right into the deep end. I've somersaulted down steps, I've drooled on my shirt, I've eaten an audience member's popcorn.* I've run laps up and down the aisle, I've carried Jeremy on my back, I've stood on my head (or have given it a valiant effort, anyway).

The sweat, the shortness of breath, even the occasional bumps and bruises, all stem from my love of total commitment to this activity. And I know the audience recognizes it. They generously offer their laughter and applause because they appreciate an improviser who leaves everything on stage.

So, to any improviser struggling with feeling ineffective on stage, I would say it's not your skill level holding you back. It's your commitment level.

Honestly, I can't imagine going about it any other way. What would be the purpose of holding back any energy, creativity, and connection on stage when those very things should characterize my performance?

You've been with me this long; you should see the improv/life metaphor forming here. I interact

---

*   Sorry, Vanessa.

with Christians who feel like their life isn't going anywhere, like God must not care. Others talk about how they haven't grown much or haven't made any connections in their church. Yet, in nearly all these cases, I see Christians who attend church once every 1.7 months, and when they do, they skirt out the door before the last song. I see Christians who let their misconceptions of the Bible being outdated, irrelevant, and confusing keep them from ever cracking it open to see for themselves.

So, to any *Christian* struggling with feeling ineffective in *life*, I would say it's not your skill level holding you back. It's your commitment level.

God calls you to love Him with all your heart, soul, and strength[1]. It's not simply because He's worthy, although that's absolutely the case. But I think God calls us to a standard of *all* because when we limit our commitment, we limit the joy and blessings that flow from a relationship with our Creator. And he wants so much joy and fulfillment for us! Jesus Himself said He "came that they may have life *and have it abundantly*" (John 10:10, ESV, emphasis mine).

But I can't stress this enough: this abundant life blossoms through your commitment and endurance through trials—not by your strength, mind you, but by trusting your Maker. James coaches us, "You know that the testing of your faith produces perseverance. Let perseverance finish its work so that you may be mature and complete, not lacking anything" (James 1:3-4, NIV). If you give half, give in, or give up, you'll miss out on the maturity, wholeness, and fulfillment Christ offers to those who persevere.

A 50% Heart

Let's look at a bizarre story from the book of 2 Kings. The prophet Elisha was on his deathbed when King Joash came to him, pleading for God's help against an incoming enemy.

> Elisha told him, "Get a bow and some arrows." And the king did as he was told. Elisha told him, "Put your hand on the bow," and Elisha laid his own hands on the king's hands. Then he commanded, "Open that eastern window," and he opened it. Then he said, "Shoot!" So he shot an arrow. Elisha proclaimed, "This is the Lord's arrow, an arrow of victory over Aram, for you will completely conquer the Arameans at Aphek." Then he said, "Now pick up the other arrows and strike them against the ground." So the king picked them up and struck the ground three times. But the man of God was angry with him. "You should have struck the ground five or six times!" he exclaimed. "Then you would have beaten Aram until it was entirely destroyed. Now you will be victorious only three times." (2 Kings 13:15-19)

Okay . . . so, on the surface, this may look like Elisha playing a tricky game of guess-a-number-from-one-to-ten.

"Uh, three?"

"Wrong! It was six. You lose!"

But the issue here was not the number. It was the heart of the king. Elisha already declared the symbolism of the arrow; it represented God's promise of victory. Next came the unspoken heart check. Would the king be energetic and emphatic given the promise? Or would a lack of faith in the promise dampen his commitment?

Remember last chapter, we read from James and saw how behavior broadcasts belief.

Your behavior demonstrates not only what you believe, but also *how strongly* you believe it.

If you say you believe, then your behaviors should support that. I want to take it a step further now.

Your behavior demonstrates not only what you believe, but also *how strongly* you believe it.

This wasn't the first time in Elisha's ministry he looked for all-in commitment. With the consequences of King Joash's half-hearted effort in mind, let's go back in time and consider the behavior of a poor widow (2 Kings 4, if you want to check it out).

A 100% Faith

This woman's husband had been a prophet friend of Elisha's. But when her husband died, she was left with two sons and, as was typical for widows in that day, no means of financial support. She owed money, and the creditor threatened to take her sons as slaves.

"What do you have?" Elisha asked.

"Nothing except a small jar of olive oil."

"Go around and ask all your neighbors for empty jars. Don't ask for just a few."

So, she did. Can you imagine the strange interactions she must have had? She knocked on her neighbor's door.

"Hello? Bethesheba?"*

"Oh! Hi, Karen!** Come on in! Oh, sorry to hear about your husband."

"Thank you, but I don't really have time to chat right now."

"Oh, okay. What can I do for you?"

"I need . . . empty jars."

"Jars? Sure. How many do you need?"

"Um . . . *all* of them?"

"*All* my jars?"

"Uh huh."

"Why—I mean, what do you need them for?"

"I . . . I'm not exactly sure."

"Okay. Will I get them back?"

"I think so?"

"Alright, dear. Take the jars. Bye now! Good to see you . . . Poor Karen. And to think she was kooky *before* her husband died!"

Door to door she went, building a new reputation as Karen the Jar Fiend. Big jars, tiny jars, clay jars, stone jars, jars under her arms and jars on her head. Finally, stockpiled with the entire village's supply of empty jars, she proceeded to

---

* Probably not her real name.

** Definitely not her real name.

do as Elisha instructed—pour oil into all the jars, and as each was filled, put it to the side.

Her sons brought her an empty jar, and she poured her little jar of oil into the big jar. The oil kept flowing until the big jar was full!

"It's still coming! Bring me the next one!" Jar after jar she filled, and the oil never stopped. Dozens of jars, now full of oil, were scattered around their small home.

"Bring me another one!"

Her sons looked around, making sure they hadn't missed one. "There's not a jar left." And only then did the oil stop flowing.

Thinking back, she must have been glad she secured every jar she possibly could. Every neighbor, every jar. Because, as she came to discover, the magnitude of the miracle was proportionate to the magnitude of her effort. And—here's the clincher—the magnitude of her effort was proportionate to the magnitude of her faith.

When she stopped pouring, the oil stopped flowing. If she had gathered two jars, and filled them to their brims, it would still have been a miracle. But we can assume it would have ended there. Fortunately, she trusted the Lord is able, through his mighty power at work within us, to accomplish infinitely more than we might ask or think[2].

If that is true of the Lord today, why are we asking or thinking for . . . I don't know. Maybe a couple of jars? We ask God for solutions we can envision ourselves and imagine circumstances quite like our current reality. And then we agonize over the idea God hasn't shown up in our lives in a dramatic way. We pray once because we feel like we should, but we stop coming to Him after a couple days of not seeing an immediate change. If this is you, the problem isn't God stopped flowing. The problem is you stopped pouring.

My encouragement to you is that even if you only poked the ground a couple of times with your victory arrows, or if you only brought one jar to the oil-pouring party, God hasn't given up on you.

> **The problem isn't God stopped flowing. The problem is you stopped pouring.**

"And I am certain that God, who began the good work within you, will continue his work until it is finally finished on the day when Christ Jesus returns" (Philippians 1:6).

God doesn't do anything half-way. Not even 99%. He will never give up on His masterpiece. He's all in. He started this work in you; you can bet your life on the fact He's going to finish it if you let Him.

A 1000% God

And, I might add, God doesn't stop at 100%, either. God is a God of generosity and abundance. In one of the most famous passages of the Bible, Psalm 23, the psalmist David paints a picture of God's generosity like a feast. "My cup overflows with blessings. Surely your goodness and unfailing love will pursue me all the days of my life, and I will live in the house of the Lord forever" (Psalm 23:5-6).

In David's culture of hospitality, the dinner host would keep the guest's cup full throughout the evening. But when the host felt like the evening was over, he would stop refilling the cup. Hint, hint, nudge, nudge. The guest should conclude it was time to call it a night—not in a mean or passive-aggressive way. That was the understanding in the culture. So, when David describes a God who not only keeps his cup full, but overflows it, he is marveling at a God who says, "I'm never sending you away. My goodness and my unfailing love will be with you forever."

Can't you hear God in all these stories pleading with us? "Come on! Bring it on! Empty yourself and I'll fill it up! Bring all the jars you can find! Don't ration the drink in your cup; I've got plenty! Try me! Go all in! I promise you won't be disappointed."

Jesus had a remarkable encounter with one woman who did take Him up on His invitation. It can be found in John 12. The implication of this story was shared with me by a pastor friend of mine, Tom Richter, and it has forever changed how I view it. I hope it inspires you as well.

Jesus was attending a party thrown in His honor. He wasn't always into the party scene, but this one was different. After all, Lazarus was there. Yes, *that* Lazarus. Recently-raised-from-the-dead Lazarus. Brother to Mary and Martha, all of them good friends of Jesus, and understandably overjoyed and thankful for how He blessed their family.

And man, was it a good time. Jesus' disciples, of course, were all invited. Bartholemew was at the turntables, mixing some "Uptown Funk." Philip clutched two handfuls of the fig cookie things Martha was passing around.

Thomas was sniffing Lazarus' skin. "It doesn't even smell dead!"

You should have been there. It was awesome.

Music, laughter, joy, dancing—everything was upbeat, fun, and celebratory. Until . . . Crash!

As with the piercing sound of shattered dishes at a restaurant, everyone stopped to look for the carnage and the embarrassed face of the guilty server.

"Martha!"

"It wasn't me! What broke out there?"

DJ Bart's needle scratched, and all went silent as they began to sniff. What was that smell? I mean, it wasn't bad, but it was super strong.

Emerging from the confused silence came the sound of sniffling. Then whimpering. Then weeping. Martha rolled her eyes.

"Mary!"

You know the person at the party who gets so swept up in everything and takes it too far, so things get awkward? Classic Mary. You see, Mary had gone to grab her jar of nard.

What? You don't have a nard jar? Oh, okay. Well, there are two things you need to know about the nard jar. First, nard was an expensive burial perfume. A pint, like Mary's, cost about a year's wages. Most people only owned one, if they owned any at all. You would save it for the death of—and this is important—your dearest loved one. Why? Because, second, it was preserved in a permanently sealed jar. You couldn't spritz it here and there like perfume nowadays. The only way to use it was to break the jar and spill it out completely, so it was a one-time deal. Afterward, it was gone. It was truly all or nothing.

So . . . why did Mary use it now? Welcome to what literally everybody in the room was thinking.

Martha, mop in hand, shrieked, "What a mess!"

Lazarus was probably like, "Wait, you didn't use that when I died?"

Judas only saw dollar signs spilling out onto the floor. "What a waste! We could have at least sold it and kept—I mean . . . *given* the money to the poor!"

Jesus finally spoke up. "Leave her alone. You'll always have poor people to take care of.

You won't always have me."

Everybody nodded solemnly. Jesus had a way of ending conversations so nobody could, in good conscience, get in the last word.

Fast forward now. You know the story. That same Judas betrayed Jesus. He was arrested, beaten, and killed. None of his friends saw it coming. They were absolutely gutted. A couple days later, it was time to go to the tomb, pay their respects, and perfume the body.

A handful of women walked together. Martha had her jar. Salome had her jar. They looked back at Mary.

"Mary did you remember to grab your—? Oh, right. I forgot . . ."

"Oh, yeah! You wasted it at that one dinner."

"Well. I bet you feel sorry now, don't you?"

Mary, empty-handed, hung her head. She *was* feeling sorry. *Maybe I was too impulsive. I didn't think about Jesus actually dying someday, and certainly not this soon. Now I don't have any way to honor Him. I love Him so much.*

Everything changed when they arrived at Jesus' tomb to find out . . . it was empty! Not only that, but Jesus was alive! Soon, they got to see Him, hug Him, and talk with Him in person again. Jesus spent a few joyous weeks with His friends before it was time for Him to go for a while. In front of a group of them, He shared His final words, and slowly rose through the clouds until He was out of sight.

Mary must have reflected on all of this, and I hope she recognized how incredibly, uniquely blessed she was. In her act of going all-in for Jesus, little did she know that of all the people at the party, of all the women to visit his tomb, she was the only one who would end up using this most prized possession the way it was intended, to honor the One who was most worthy. Nobody else would have the chance to honor Him like she did.

Imagine Martha. She returned home from the empty tomb with her jar of nard still intact. She held it for a moment thoughtfully before returning it to its shelf. And there it sat. Years passed, and I wonder if that jar didn't serve as a constant reminder to Martha of what could have been?

If *work* hadn't come before *worship*, maybe she would have realized a life spent pouring is a life without regret.

—~m~—

In this unscripted life, not fully committing to your scene—your relationship with your Heavenly Father—may feel like you're protecting yourself. After all, you don't know what's going to happen. And if you're not entirely committed, then you can't be entirely disappointed, right?

And so, you hedge your bets. Instead of breaking open the jar in total commitment, you treat your involvement like a spray bottle. A spritz here. Maybe this will work out. But God has disappointed me in this area before, so I don't want to get my hopes up again. A spritz there. I can handle this myself.

But, my friend, a relationship with God is what you were created for. The more of your heart, soul, and strength you pour into it, the more He will fill you up with what you truly need.

Anything less than *all* is only robbing yourself of infinitely more than you can ask or imagine.

End Scene!

And so, my friend, the curtain drops on the end of our conversation for now. I truly hope these pages have inspired a shift of thought, mindset, or behavior. I look forward to hearing how God uses this to invite you closer to Him.

I'd like to issue one warning, however. If you lean in and invite God to help you become a *Relationship-Builder, Problem-Solver, Pace-Setter, Truth-Teller, Action-Taker,* and *All-Giver,* then you should prepare to be interrupted. Get ready for opportunities to put these new skills to the test.

In the time I spent writing this book, I experienced unexpected financial burdens, nagging illnesses, friends with struggling marriages, the death of a family member, even the unprecedented COVID-19 crisis that threw the entire world off script. Each curveball thrown and carpet yanked from underfoot forced me to go back to what I knew to be true from God's word, and what I was sharing in this book. I still don't know all the *why*s of those events, but I am confident God is near, He cares, and He wants us to walk through them together.

Never stop improv-ing.

ACKNOWLEDGMENTS

Before I even started contemplating writing a book, I thought, "Man, if I ever write a book, I'm going to skip over the acknowledgments and preface and introduction and junk and get right to the good stuff!" Well, I still feel the same way about the preface and introduction (you're welcome), but I simply couldn't wrap this up without taking the opportunity to honor some of the amazing individuals who were fountains for me and this book.

My wife Kelsey, who deserves an entire book's worth of acknowledgment for her support.

My daughter Adalynne, who asked me to read unfinished chapters at bedtime, and not just to stay up later.

Mom and Dad, from whom I learned the Bible cover to cover in an interactive and memorable way.

Carl and Jeremy of 321 Improv, with whom it has been an honor to share the stage and to call friends.

A bevy of amazing men of God who have generously given me opportunities to grow creatively in the church, and whom I am blessed to have been able to call *pastor*—David Nasser, Tom Gerdts, Pablo Lopez, and Josh Gagnon.

Kary Oberbrunner and the Igniting Souls Tribe, who have made this process a joy.

My Next Level Church family, whose support is ecstatic and unwavering.

The author of my story, Jesus Christ. Please make much of Yourself through this book.

Credit to some much smarter people!

Chapter 3
[1] From a 1943 letter by C.S. Lewis, included in *Yours, Jack: Spiritual Direction from C.S. Lewis.*
[2] Bonhoeffer, Dietrich. *Life Together: The Classic Exploration of Christian in Community.* Harper One, 2009, p. 99.

Chapter 4
[1] Interview by Rick Bommelje, "Listening Post," Summer 2003, Vol 84.
[2] Covey, Stephen R. *The 7 Habits of Highly Effective People: Restoring the Character Ethic.* [Rev. ed.]. New York: Free Press, 2004, p. 235.

Chapter 7
[1] Hull, Bill. *The Complete Book of Discipleship: On Being and Making Followers of Christ.* NavPress, 2006, p. 122.

Chapter 10
[1] Halpern, Charna, Del Close, and Kim Johnson. *Truth in Comedy: The Manual of Improvisation.* Colorado Springs, Colorado: Meriwether Pub., 1994, p. 15.

Chapter 11
[1] Numbers 9:17
[2] Exodus 34:29
[3] Jakes, TD. *10 Commandments of Christian Leadership.* C3 Conference, Dallas, Texas, 2007.

Chapter 12
  [1] Deuteronomy 6:5
  [2] Ephesians 3:20

ABOUT THE AUTHOR

Mike Domeny joined 321 Improv in 2011, bringing his brand of energy and connection to hundreds of thousands across the country. Since 2016, he has served as a creative writer for Next Level Church, as well as a creative consultant for other churches. Using the principles in this book, he also coaches individuals and teams to increase their adaptability when dealing with the unexpected. Mike and his wife, Kelsey, raise their daughter Adalynne in New Hampshire.

Did you enjoy the book?

I hope this book offered value to your life. If you believe someone else could benefit from the concepts in this book, I encourage you to leave a review of this book at your favorite online retailer.

Raise Your A.Q. (Adaptability Quotient)

If you enjoyed the tips and concepts in this book, you'll love taking them to the next level with the Thrown Off Script Training Course. Assess your Adaptability Quotient and interact with improv principles and biblical truths through fun, engaging games and exercises. Ideal for a small group video study, or live facilitator-led workshops.

Raise your A.Q. and thrive off script today!

MikeDomeny.com

Bring Mike to your church, organization, or event.

Mike knows the importance of choosing the right speaker for your event. You need someone you can trust to deliver memorable and high-quality content, to connect with your audience on stage and off, and to serve your event with the professionalism and integrity it deserves.

Mike's genuine approach and premier content makes him a top choice for many organizations and events.

Bring Mike and his conversational, energetic, humorous-yet-poignant style to your stage. He customizes each message and training to fit your theme and exceed your goals.

Contact Mike today and start the conversation.

MikeDomeny.com

CPSIA information can be obtained
at www.ICGtesting.com
Printed in the USA
BVHW071941240620
582044BV00005B/99

9 781647 461539